Kayla's Story:
GOING HOME EARLY

ANNETTE WATSON

WestBow
PRESS
A DIVISION OF THOMAS NELSON

WestBow Press books may be ordered through booksellers or by contacting:

WestBow Press
A Division of Thomas Nelson
1663 Liberty Drive
Bloomington, IN 47403
www.westbowpress.com
1-(866) 928-1240

ISBN: 978-1-4497-9227-5 (sc)
ISBN: 978-1-4497-9228-2 (hc)
ISBN: 978-1-4497-9226-8 (e)

Library of Congress Control Number: 2013907305

Printed in the United States of America.

WestBow Press rev. date: 04/25/2013

This book is dedicated to all of those in our small community of Atoka who have lost children. The list is far too long for a town of our small population. I admire your courage to continue to find hope and life beyond your loss. I pray this book helps in healing your hearts.

"The memory of the righteous is blessed."
(Proverbs 10:7)

TABLE OF CONTENTS

FOREWORD

Kayla was a very unique person. I had the privilege of being her pastor, but more importantly, she was a spiritual daughter to me. I loved her just like she was my own. I never met anyone who ever had one negative thing to say about Kayla. Everyone loved her and she loved everyone she met, always seeing the best in them.

Kayla was an amazing basketball player, but her legacy lives in the type of person she was. She lived her life fully out of love. This book will give you her perspective on life and will touch the very core of your being. You will read how she lived life to the fullest and how she tried to show the love of the Father to everyone she met.

I do not have words for the respect I have for the Watson family and how they have dealt with Kayla going home early. I can't imagine losing a child or the pain they have suffered. I know they have made Kayla proud of how they continue to live their lives and trust Father God in all things.

May this book give you, the reader, just a glimpse of the greatness of Kayla Watson, and to all of us that had the privilege of knowing her. We are all better people!

Darrin Begley

PREFACE

December 2012

My mom was taking my cousin, Reta Watson out for her birthday. I love my cousin, Reta; she has always been so special to me. She has been so helpful to my mom since my loss. Her daughter, Emily, sang at my service. Emily used to come to my house and I would make her sing to me. She would sing, "It's going to be worth it, it's going to be worth it." It truly was Emily. I love Reta and I am happy that so many years ago I invited her to start attending my church, God's House. It was just like Reta to play a huge part in the writing of this book. It was her birthday and Mom said, "You pick what you want to do". She gave her the option of going to watch Gerard Butler's new movie, but Reta told her that Pastor Darrin was speaking at a church in Ardmore and she would like to go hear him. They were so excited to get hear him speak again. They passed on Gerard Butler and got to have a divine encounter with God. Pastor Darrin told my mom at that service, "You think you just love books because you like to read, but God says you have a book in you and it is time to write." Now, my mom was going to obey God just at that word, but a couple of days later God sends confirmation when another Pastor, Larry Luman, had a chance encounter with her at my dad's taxidermy shop. She didn't know that Larry was there and had gone out to take care of some business for my dad. She visited briefly with Larry and he told her how much they were enjoying pastoring their new church since leaving God's House. After visiting a few minutes, Mom walked off and Larry stopped her and said, "You need to write a book." He had not been at the service at Ardmore and had no way of knowing the words that Pastor Darrin had already spoken. Mom as usual was quick to obey God and began writing this book about me. At that time, it had been seven years since my death. The timing was perfect for the book. As my dad told her, "Seven years is God's number for completion and perfection in the bible." The words poured out of her effortlessly as God's grace was upon her to write.

My family has survived the most overwhelming blow that they could experience and have come out stronger in their faith and walk with God. No, they did not get over my death, but they did get *beyond it* by the grace of God. Yes, they still grieve for the loss, but not as those who have no hope (1 Thessalonians 4:13).

This book is based on the writings I had left behind and my mom's letters, notes, and journals following my death.

ACKNOWLEDGEMENT

I want to thank all of the people who encouraged me on this journey to remember Kayla. Thank you to all of my Facebook© friends who supported me and made me believe that our story could help heal and inspire others.

I would like to especially thank Angela Bagby for her time and dedication spent on the editing of this book. She was a lifesaver and I am so thankful for her. She freely gave me the gift of editing my book and this was a huge task. I hope someday I can repay the favor.

Thank you to Brad Buttry for the graphic design. You gave me the priceless gift of creating a family picture of my children after Kayla had died. It is one of my greatest treasures. And now for the book cover you perfectly captured my daughter's beauty. You continue to amaze me with your ability and your generosity.

I want to thank those who walked through the valley of the shadow of death with me. My friend, Laura Durbin, worked beside me every day and helped me through so many hard times. Laura's way of dealing with death is avoidance, but because of our friendship she was willing not only to walk with me at the time of Kayla's death, but also again when I started writing the book. Thank you, Laura.

Shelly Pond, who coached my daughter and became my friend, you were so much more than a coach to Kayla. She loved you so much. You allowed her to be herself and embraced her love. I have been around college basketball enough to know that caring for kids beyond the court is a rare gift. I love you for making her happy. We will forever be bonded together by the love and loss of "our" Kayla.

Thank you to my pastors, Darrin and Sheila Begley for your profound influence on my daughter's life. She loved you guys so much and wanted everyone to come to her church to experience God. This book is a result of you teaching us to hear God's voice and to dare to obey.

Most of all thank you to my heavenly Father who chose me to be the typist for one of His stories.

Annette Watson

MY BIRTH

"The thief comes to steal, kill, and destroy . . ."
(John 10:10)

The first attack on my life came while I was still in the womb. The enemy tried to kill me then. He knew that I was going to be a passionate servant of God so he tried to take me out early. My mom was only 28 weeks in gestation and she went for her six month check up. When Mom was lying on the table waiting for the doctor, she felt a strange sensation and wondered if her water had broke. She panicked when she looked up to see her white pants soaked in blood. She started screaming and the doctor and nurse ran into the room. Mom was immediately rushed to the hospital. They were talking about taking me and my mom was scared to death, not realizing that babies could survive on their own, even at 28 weeks. Mom was given some medicine to stop the bleeding and contractions. After a few days in the hospital, she was sent home with orders for complete bed rest. Two weeks later, we had the same situation and she was rushed by ambulance to Baylor Medical Center in Dallas, Texas, where there was a special care nursery and I would have a better chance of survival. Poor Mom! She went through all the labor pains in the ambulance and was completely dilated without any pain medication. The nurses were helping her and yelling for the driver to hurry. Mom would have given birth to me in the ambulance, but I was turned sideways. So, even though she has suffered through all the pain, they have to do cesarean-section to deliver me. I was born eleven minutes after Mom arrived at the hospital.

My dad missed my birth because the doctors had told him that they were going to prolong my delivery by giving Mom some medication that would stop the labor. They told him it would be a few days before I was born. So, Dad went home to get clothes and make preparations. These were the days before cell phones so he had no communication with us until he arrived at the hospital, three hours after my birth, to be told that mother and DAUGHTER were fine. I weighed in at a whopping 3.2 pounds. Frighteningly, my first night, I lost 13 ounces and weighed only 2.5 pounds by morning. Mom and Dad couldn't hold me because I was so small and fragile, but, amazingly, my lungs were developed. My parents had to look at me through the glass of the incubator. They were so worried, but the little girl next to me only weighed 1.8 pounds, and had survived open heart surgery so I liked my odds. I had to stay in the hospital for five weeks before I could come home.

Mom and Dad didn't name me for almost a week. Remember, I was born at six and a half months. They thought they would have plenty of time to pick out a name. A name can be prophetic. Mom and Dad wanted a name that would speak into my life and help form my identity. I think they got it right. Kayla means "pure." I tried to live holy and, most importantly, I tried to live with a pure heart. That doesn't mean that I was perfect, but my name was prophetic and an accurate description of me. I was called from the womb to do the work of God. Just like we all are. God has a purpose and a plan for each of us. We are all called for his purpose, but He is a gentleman. He won't force us to serve him. He lets us choose. I chose to follow.

Mom was released from Baylor after a week and I was transferred to Texoma Medical Center (TMC) in Denison, Texas, which was much closer to home. I stayed here another month. Each morning before Mom got on the road to the hospital she called to see what I weighed. Mom and Dad were so anxious to have me home, but I couldn't be released from the hospital until I weighed five pounds. Other than a little jaundice, I didn't have any medical problems except my low birth weight. What a miracle! Every day, Mom would come to the hospital and sit by my incubator. She got to hold me about an hour a day and the rest of the time she would touch me through a hole in the incubator. Even then, I would grip her hand with my fingers and hold on tightly. I know the doctors were concerned about bonding because Mom couldn't hold me much or nurse me. In fact, I didn't even have the instinct to suck because of my premature birth. Mom and Dad were so excited when I would take even an ounce of milk. There was no need to worry about our bond; however, Mom and I loved each other from the moment of conception. Just as I latched on to her hand with my little fingers, we would cling together for the rest of my life. In fact, long after I had outgrown "sleeping in the middle," I would sleep on the floor by Mom's bedside and she would hold my hand until I was sound asleep.

My dad splurged and spent some of his last money on a "Smurf" from the hospital gift shop to leave in my incubator when he had to leave to go back to work. I kept this "Smurf" the rest of my life. Twenty-one years later, my dad would put it in my casket. We had gone full circle.

After five weeks, I reached four pounds and four ounces and the doctor released me to go home. There was a slight problem from the hospital stay. I completely had my days and my nights mixed up, as nurses on the night shift played with me all night, and usually the day shift nurses were too busy. Those nurses were so sad when I left them; we had gotten attached. The mix up with my days and nights were so bad that I would keep my mom up all night the first nine months of my life.

Doctors had warned my parents that I would likely be delayed in life and would not excel, so they should not have high expectations for me. My parents never accepted this negative report. Yes, I was a little delayed in walking and talking. I didn't crawl until I was ten months old and I didn't take my first step until I was thirteen months old. I got my first tooth at 14 months. My mom said I was always a very well mannered and obedient child. As a toddler, I learned what "no" meant really quickly when Mom slapped my hands. I was easy to toilet train. The major problem I had during this time was giving up my bottle. I was really attached to that thing. My mom was going to college at the time and would often stay up all night listening to me cry for my bottle. She would survive the night, only to have my papa (Jack Rose) babysit me while she attended class the next day. I could always talk him into giving it back to me. She finally put up a big enough fuss and conspired to have everyone, including him, keep it from me.

At age 2, I was completely adorable and the center of my parent's world. I had big brown eyes with a round, chubby face and brown, curly hair. My mom didn't work outside of the home while I was young, which allowed me to have her full attention. I was my mom's helper and my dad's best hunting buddy, but my whole world was about to be invaded.

When I was 3 years old, I was introduced to my brother, Matthew Kyle Watson, and I got my first lesson in sharing (my parents). How dare he take all the attention? I adjusted and grew to actually be tolerant of him. My Nan's spanking probably helped the adjustment. Again, Matt's name was carefully chosen and means "gift from God." There was no better way to describe Matt than being our gift. Mom was able to carry him full term, but was terribly sick and hospitalized three times during the pregnancy. Matt weighed 7 and ½ pounds which was nearly half-grown compared to me. I was a little jealous at first, but took to being a big sister quickly. We became playmates. Cassie, my cousin who was born five days before me, lived a mile away and we were close playmates. Matt, Cassie and I played together almost every day. We played "school" every day. We baked cookies. We watched movies. I am so thankful Mom got to be a stay-at-home Mom. She applied for a job at the Oklahoma Department of Human Services since she had completed her Bachelor's Degree in Sociology at Southeastern Oklahoma State University in Durant, Oklahoma, right before Matt was born. She didn't get that job which frustrated her because we needed the money. She would often feel so discouraged when she wouldn't be chosen after an interview. She was born to be a social worker, but couldn't get a job. She didn't realize that it wasn't God's timing and that He was giving her that precious time with her kids and that one day she would look back and realize that his failure to answer her prayer for a job was in fact His way of blessing her with time with me.

Matt and I loved to go to our nana and papa's house and they were always happy to have us. They came by every day after work to see us. No matter what their plans were, they would immediately change if we wanted to come over. They played with us all the time. Those were such happy times. I stayed close with Nan (Shirley) all my life. I taught her how to email me once I was in college so we could stay close and every Sunday, without fail, I would call her to check on her.

Matt and I had so much fun as kids. We played so hard. We played basketball for hours, jumped on our trampoline, built tree houses or would just sit for hours drawing "Rugrats" and "Simpson" characters. I wrote this poem about Matt when I was in high school.

When my little brother was born
I didn't know what to do
I didn't like all the fussle and bussle made on his every move
I wanted to hold him and love him and stuff
But when I got through with him that was enough
I wanted for myself all the attention
And this little boy's birth caused a lot of dissension
But I learned to live with it
And now can see that the little boy's birth was great thing for me

Matt and I really never had much trouble, except on ball court. We were both born with that dominant, competitive gene that all Watsons possess. If I could go back now, I would probably let him win some, lol. He was such a competitor and he hated to lose. Once, when we were in high school, we were playing basketball on our court at home. I beat him ten times in a row in the game of "21." He would get so mad and he would say, "Play me again." I had a height advantage on him and he couldn't get a rebound. He would get close to beating me, but never would, especially this particular day. Finally, I grew tired of playing and he was mad that I wanted to quit playing. He kept saying, "One more game! I will beat you this time," but I was tired so I went in the house. He came in and told Mom, "Make her play me again. She won't play me because she knows I will beat her." Seriously, Matt I just beat you ten times in a row, but you are so sure you can win the next one. He got a double dose of that competitive gene that the all of the Watsons have. I didn't play him again. Mom said, "Kayla just let him win once," but I refused because I would never hear the end of it from him.

The summer following my graduation from high school I was going to be leader at church camp and the pre-camp trainer suggested we write a letter to someone who meant more to us than we had let them know. I chose to write to my baby brother, but I didn't give it to him yet. It wasn't time. It wouldn't mean as much until after my death. In fact, it was seven years later when mom when they were going through my belongings getting material for this book that he found the letter. It was perfect timing. He was now a parent and I knew he was ready. My letter was a treasure to him and he took it the next day to his safety deposit box for safe keeping.

Matt,

The teacher of our conference for EM (church) told us to write a letter to someone who was very important to us, but we didn't let them know that enough. So, I knew I should write my letter to you. I know I never tell you how much you mean to me and how much I love you. Pretty soon, we will be getting a new brother and I hope that in no way I ever make you feel like I love him more. I know it probably seemed like when you would get in arguments with people at school that I was on their side and I'm so sorry if I made you feel that way. I know it must be hard following in my shadow because of me being the basketball player and the bible club leader and all of that, but never feel like you are just in my shadow because that was not true. You can do so much more than me. God has his own plan for your life too and there are people that only you can touch and show them Jesus. Never let anything come before God. Always keep him #1 and don't be content with just being a Christian. Run after God with all of your heart Matt. Even as your name means "gift of God" that was the way you are to me and to Mom and Dad and to so many others. Please forgive me for not showing you or telling you enough how much you mean to me . . . Kay

My sweet little brother grew up to be such a good man. He married my friend, Monise Huskey. He fell in love with her in the ninth grade, when she moved to Tushka from Oregon. He asked her out every single day. He finally wore her down when they were seniors. They started dating a few months after I left for heaven. She was perfect for him and she helped him through the grief. He was just like Dad. He has high moral standards. I was and still am so proud of him. He has never once drank or done drugs. He takes those sweet little nieces of mine to church and has been dedicated to raising Godly daughters. I could not be more proud of him. I remember when he proposed to Monise. He told her, "Now, if you marry me you are going to be stuck in Caney, because I am never leaving Mom. She has lost one kid and I am always going to be there for her." Monise didn't mind a bit. She loves Mom too. I know me and Mo would be best of friends if I were still there.

At age four, I was a chatterbox and would have this circular conversation with my mom where I would say, "Hey, Mom!" She would say, "Yes." I would say, "Guess what?" She would say, "What?" I would say, "I love you." She would say, "I love you, too." I would do this over and over, at least 50 times a day. My mom would play along for a while, but then she would say, "Let's rest our ears, awhile," or "Let's don't tell Mom so much." She told me about this later in life and I would do it just to aggravate her. My dad would later tell Mom that I was just making up for all the times I wouldn't be there after my death to tell her.

ELEMENTARY SCHOOL— CANEY YEARS

I stayed home with my mom until I went to school. When I was six, I began school at Caney. Ms. Harbin was my Kindergarten teacher. My first day of school was traumatic. My mom had not worked outside of the home. She had gone to college and I had stayed with my grandparents, but I really had not been away from my mom much. I cried and cried because I didn't want her to leave me there. Ms. Harbin let me sit by Cassie and that made me feel better. I soon adjusted and learned to like school. We learned the alphabet with "letter people" and learned some goofy songs like, "The Crazy Old Man from China." I would come home and teach these to Matt every day. Matt was having a hard time, too. He cried when I went to school. He wanted to go with me. Once, he even loaded up on the bus and Mom had to climb on the bus to get him. She played with him and they baked cookies for me to eat when I got home. He told Mom, "Sometimes, I just need some lovings." She always had plenty. He would also tell her he wanted to "Eat at fried tucky" referring to Kentucky Fried Chicken (KFC). He also liked to get a "hot chocolate Sunday." We laughed about how he said things when we were young. Matt loved Mom's homemade chocolate chip cookies and she would always tell him, "I know that no matter how old you get and how far away you might move, all I have to do is bake some cookies to keep you coming home." It was actually her deer meat that he would always want her to cook after he was grown. I loved for her to cook deer meat, too, and would have her bring it to me at college. She and Dad would get up and cook me fresh deer meat before making the four hour trip to my games.

Starting Kindergarten was a huge transition for me, like I said, because I had not been away from Mom much and I hated leaving her. She would take me to school and I would tell her I loved her before getting out of the car. Paula Huffman had taught me the American Sign Language (ASL) deaf sign for I love you and I used it the rest of my life. As I walked to my kindergarten class, I would hold my hand behind my back making the "I love you" sign for Mom to see all the way to my classroom. I also had a little "Winnie-the-Pooh" doll that I had got for my 6th birthday and I put him in my backpack every day to go to school with me. Ms. McBride was my teacher in first grade. We were learning math and had math races. My competitive nature was becoming evident, even back then. Each day I would come home and tell Mom what I placed in the math race. Cassie was always faster than me and I remember once telling her "faster does not mean smarter."

We had such a large number of students in our class that in second grade they split our classes. Initially, Ms. Workman was my teacher and I was in the same class as Cassie. I was often sad and discouraged because she could beat me in the math race. Mom decided to move me to the other class where she thought I would concentrate more on learning than winning. Ms. Mitchell was my teacher and she was so sweet. My mom even volunteered one day a week to help her grade papers and stuff. It was fun having her there. I was beginning to come out of my shell and shocked everyone when Ms. Mitchell was bent over and I smacked her on the behind. Ms. Mitchell just laughed and said "I can't believe you did that, Kayla." It was funny, but I never tried that again. I got my first three-wheeler at this time. Cassie got one, too, and we spent a lot of time riding together. We played together nearly every afternoon. If we were not riding three-wheelers, we were playing "McDonalds" in my new playhouse that Dad had built me for my birthday. It had a window on each side so we had a drive through, play food, and everything. Cassie and I also played soccer that year and our coach called us the "Dynamic Duo."

Another important change had occurred in my life; my mom went to work at DHS. This was real hard for me because she had always been home after school. Now, I had to go to a babysitter after school. Oh yeah, I got my first kiss in second grade when Chance Crites kissed me on the forehead at the Halloween party.

In third grade, my little brother, Matt joined me at school when he began Kindergarten. I enjoyed being the big sister and always walked him to his building before going to my class. One of the highlights of the year was when I won the Halloween costume contest when I dressed up as cat woman. Ms. McBride was my teacher again and I always liked her. I got student of the month once and I also got my first "B" which made me cry. In third grade, I started playing Little Dribblers basketball, but soon quit because basketball just wasn't my thing. Isn't that ironic?

By fourth grade, I had overcome some of my shyness and was developing into quite a tomboy. Cassie, Matt, and I spent many days building forts, playing in the tree house and riding bikes. Cassie was always bigger than me and I remember that she had this huge adult bicycle with a big banana seat and she could just zip around on it. I had this small pink bike with training wheels. I would often cry because Cassie could go faster than me.

Ms. Haddock was my fourth grade teacher and I made a "B" for the second time in my life. The grade upset me, not because of pressure from my parents to make straight "A's," but because I am competitive and I always wanted to be my best. I worked hard in the classroom. As a senior in high school, I had the honor of being class salutatorian. My principal, Mr. Simpson, told Mom that I would be successful even if I didn't have basketball scholarship because I had the same work ethic in class. So, in fourth grade, I brought the grade up by the end of the semester so no damage was done. I also started playing coach-pitch softball that summer.

One thing I recall about fifth grade was that I started playing basketball again. Ms. McBride was our coach. Ms. Carroll was my teacher in fifth grade. She was very sweet and I really liked her. We also had a practice teacher, Miss Sewell, whom I loved. I always loved Miss Sewell. She came to my games when I was in high school and I was so excited she was there. I always had a smile and a hug for her.

In the sixth grade, I finally got to have Ms. Gray for my teacher. She was the sweetest person. She was always smiling and encouraging. She made me feel special, but, then, so did all the rest. She was a gifted teacher. I had to get braces that year. I really needed them because my teeth were terribly crooked and other kids made fun of them. I remember being in a crowd of friends and someone saying, "Look at Kayla's teeth." I was so embarrassed. I was happy to get braces and realized that someday I would have a beautiful smile.

That summer our twelve-and-under softball team advanced to the National Tournament in Alabama. Even though we got beat out by losing the first two games, the trip was a lot of fun. We also went to Tennessee during my sixth grade year to watch Cassie's older sister, Lari Ann, play in the National Finals. Lari played at SOSU with Crystal Robinson, who played in the WNBA after college. I loved watching Lari and her team. They were so good and got runner up in the National Championship, losing by one point. I was really starting to get into sports at this point in my life. Another exciting thing that summer was when Matt and I got a trampoline and we would spend hours together learning new tricks. We loved the outdoors.

MIDDLE SCHOOL—
STRINGTOWN YEARS

A few things happened in seventh grade that would alter the course of my life. First of all, I was experiencing a really hard time at school. I had no friends. No one would talk to me or sit by me in the lunch room or on the playground. It was very cliquish. If you were this girl's friend, you couldn't talk to this other girl. Normal girl drama, I guess, but I was sensitive. This had occurred at different times during my school life, but it became intense in seventh grade. Looking back now, I know it was meant to be. I now know that it was a part of the plan. See, I needed to go to other schools so I could have more friends to influence. The enemy meant it for evil, but God brought good from it. I would have relationships at Caney, Stringtown, and Tushka.

Stringtown was so important in my life because this was where I got a sense of belonging and acceptance. I don't know what would have happened if I had stayed at Caney where I often felt that I was without friends. Another good thing that came from this experience was that I was always very responsive and caring to people who didn't have friends. I was drawn to the ones that everyone else would overlook and ignore. I always looked for the outcasts and the loners. When I went into the cafeteria I looked for someone sitting alone and befriended them.

I had often asked Mom about changing schools. She always wanted to pray about it and believed that things would get better. She always tried to make things better. She would take me to fun places like the park and "Discovery Zone." I was happy at home, but at school I was miserable. It really got my mom's attention one day when I was really sick, but begged to go to school and I finally told Mom that if I missed school the other girls would get my only friend, Mindy, and I would lose her, too. This broke my mother's heart and she said, "That is it! We are changing schools." This was the turning point in my life.

I had planned to go to Tushka since it was closer to our home and Mom would have to drive me every day, but the elementary principal said no because I didn't live in the school district. Anyway, it all worked out for the best because I ended up at Stringtown. I loved Stringtown and everything about it. I had tons of friends the very first day. Toni, Shelli, Audrey, Jamie, Melissa, Leah and all of us became one big happy group. There were no cliques and no one was left out. Melissa Isom was my step-cousin and we became very close friends. She practically lived with us. It was such a happy time in my life. I will always love Stringtown and appreciate how important they were in my life.

In fact, I loved Stringtown so much that I talked Mom and Dad into letting me go back for 8th grade. This was a sacrifice because Mom had to drive me to school and pick me up which was hard with her work schedule, but, to her, it was worth it.

One of my funniest memories from school is when Shelli sang her new song with the "bible ladies." The "bible ladies" came every week and they had a guitar and would sing. Melissa and I dared Shelli Reeves to make up a song and sing for them. I don't know how she kept from laughing because Melissa and I sure couldn't. She made it through though and the "bible ladies" commended her for the song.

When I was in the seventh grade, we had a car accident. My mom was driving my brother and me to Oklahoma City to go shopping. My mom was a terrible driver, especially at night or in the rain, and she rear-ended the vehicle in front of her, resulting in a three-car collision. Mom and I were fine, but Matt wasn't. He was bleeding badly from his head. It was chaos and yet my mom stayed calm. The first thing she did was pray with us. Afterwards, she began checking on the other people in the accident and called for an ambulance. I was so worried about Matt's bleeding head that I took off one of his socks and made a compression for the gash on his head. He asked me if he was dying. There was blood all over his face and he was crying. I tried to keep him calm; and Mom continued to check on us, too. Finally, the ambulance came and we took Matt to the emergency room where he got twelve stitches just above his eye. We were so thankful that no one was seriously injured. Matt and I would, from that day, hate to ride with Mom if it was raining.

My papa, Jack Rose, would come get us from school, sometimes, when Mom was unable. One day he let me drive home from Stringtown. My dad was in shock when we drove up in the yard. He asked papa, "What is going on?" He was thinking that maybe Papa had let me drive just from Voca Road, but my papa said, "No, she drove all way from Stringtown. She was a good little driver, I would not be afraid to let her drive me anywhere." My dad said, "She is just 14 she can't be driving."

During eighth grade, I had my first experience with death when my papa died. He was the one who always gave my bottle back to me. The night before he died, he said that he wished he could live so he could watch me play basketball. He was my greatest fan. I am so thankful that he gave his life to God just the year before he passed so we had the comfort of knowing he was in heaven and we would see him again someday. He was supposed to go to the revival with us that night, but Mom couldn't get him on the phone. She sensed something was wrong and asked a friend to go by and check on him. He called back with the news that Papa was gone. He had a massive heart attack. He was only 59 years old. We rushed to his house. Mom called her brothers, Mick and Sam, who met us there. Mom was so upset. She was close to Papa. He had lived with us several times during his illness. Papa was apparently trying to make it to the bathroom to pull the chain for help when he died. Dad wouldn't let Mom see him like that. He didn't want her to have that memory. Mom was crying hysterically. My dad can't stand to not be able to take care of her. I remember him trying to take care of arrangements, but trying to comfort Mom, too. Dad went to the porch, found Mom and started crying himself, saying "I loved him, too." Then we all gathered together, held hands, and prayed. Then we did what we always do. We went on to church. The whole family, including my uncles, went on to the revival. We poured out our hearts to God at church and found comfort in His presence. My mom would mourn for my papa every day. She would cry every day for him for a long time.

It was also during this year that I really started to develop my basketball skills. I was fast and could beat anyone down the floor for a lay-up. I remember scoring 24 points against Tushka.

HIGH SCHOOL—TUSHKA YEARS

I began ninth grade at Stringtown. During a softball game, I met and became close friends with Emily Eaves. She wanted me to come to Tushka to play basketball with them. I had already started school at Stringtown. It was such a difficult decision. I loved all of my Stringtown friends and didn't want to leave, but it was still a long drive and my mom always had to juggle her schedule to pick me and Matt up. We would have to wait on her a long time, sometimes, because of her demanding job and crazy work hours. Transportation was an issue and there was the fact that Rick Bowen who was my coach at Stringtown had left and moved to Tushka. I was fond of him. He was a good coach. Now, we would be getting a coach I didn't know. Plus, there was basketball to consider. Tushka's basketball team was very good and this was a great opportunity for me. So, I moved in October of my freshman year. Tushka welcomed me just like Stringtown had and, in fact, my first day there I was elected as a homecoming candidate for our freshman class. I was immediately accepted by the school I would love and would love me so much in return.

I had a very good life. I got to live every little girl's dream. I was homecoming candidate every one of my high school years and my senior year I was nominated to represent the girls' basketball team. I really didn't know if I would win. I had heard a lot of talk about how the honor should go to someone who had gone to Tushka their whole life and I was an interloper here having only attended since my freshman year. I know most girls make a big fuss about their dress and all. Of course, I wanted to look pretty, but I didn't want to spend a lot of money doing it. My aunt, Laura Durbin, would always do my makeup and Vickie Hall would work her magic on my hair otherwise known as my "busted bale of hay." I didn't need an expensive dress, but my mom insisted we go dress shopping and that I get a nice dress. So, my mom, Aunt Laura, and I went to Oklahoma City on a Saturday to shop for a dress. As usual, Mom had a foster child she had to stop and see at a hospital so we stopped there before hitting the mall. Aunt Laura was driving my mom's car and out of habit she locks the door with the keys still in the vehicle. Out of habit, she planned to use the keypad on the outside of the door. The problem was my mom had never known her door code. Now, we were stuck. Mom said we just needed to call a locksmith and went on into the hospital. Aunt Laura and I worked furiously trying to figure out the door code. We prayed and punched the numbers until, miraculously, the door unlocked. We were punching so fast we didn't even know what numbers we had put in. The door key pad has never worked again, but it worked that once. Oh, the shouting and laughter in the parking lot that day. We saved big by not calling a locksmith. We went on to the mall where I found a maroon dress that was perfect and cost 20 bucks. Aunt Laura said that I could make any dress look like a million bucks. I still wasn't sure that I would win. In fact, I seriously doubted that I would, but my little brother's freshman class sealed the deal. There were 38 in his class and 37 voted for me. I won the title of Homecoming Queen. Chance was my escort. He was so nervous. He kissed me on the cheek three times before the cameras finally caught it.

My experience at Tushka was wonderful. I felt accepted. I felt welcomed. I missed my Stringtown friends and hoped they would forgive me for leaving. You see, I had other lives to touch. My steps were ordered of the Lord.

CHURCH

*"And they devoted themselves to the apostles' teaching
and the fellowship, to the breaking of bread and the prayers."*
(Acts 2:42)

My mom always loved God and my dad had, too, but after his first marriage ended in divorce he quit going to church. You see, my dad was married before and he had a daughter, Kary Jo, who was my half sister. She was three, when they divorced and it hurt my dad. He was so distraught after losing Kary that he would seek medication just to help him get through it. He ended up out of the church and I guess disappointed with God. After my birth, my mom wanted to do things right and she knew that I needed to know God. Shortly after I was born, we began getting visitors from the Pentecostal Holiness Church in Caney where my dad was raised and attended before going through the divorce. Alfred and Mattie Winters were the pastors there and they would come to see us often. They invited my mom to a revival that Farron Oliver was preaching. Mom had gone to church there occasionally with Dad when they we were dating, but, now, she was a Mom and she knew I was a blessing from God. She wanted me raised in church. She went to the revival and recommitted her life to the Lord. Guess what, Mom, you got it right! I would often write Mom cards when I was older and tell her how thankful I was to have been raised in a Christian home.

Mattie and Alfred Winters were such Godly examples. They were spiritual parents to my mom and dad. They would disciple my mom and ground her in the word of God. Mattie and Alfred really enjoyed me, too. In fact, when I was about a year old Mattie taught me to praise the Lord. Mom still has pictures of me with arms outstretched while Mattie sang to me songs about God. My dad didn't go to church with us at first. My mom was so burdened for him because she wanted both of them to serve God and raise their kids to know God. Mom would sit throughout services and just weep before God and pray for my dad to be saved. One night Mom and I rode with Mattie and Alfred to a revival in Atoka at a Pentecostal Holiness church and Mom felt such a burden for my dad. She was in deep sorrow. She just couldn't quit crying; she was so burdened for my dad to return to the Lord. He had not come with us to church, but during the service while she was praying and crying he came in and went to the altar. Praise God. We were so happy. We were now united in our faith and service to God. Our faith would become the cornerstone of our family. We would meet so many wonderful people at church. Donnie and Marsha Collins were also our pastors and, of course, lifelong friends. We attended church and became close friends with Darla and Harold Delay, Oren and Eula Cochran, and Barbara and Milford Powell who would also experience the heartbreak of losing a child.

Although I had grown up in church, I had not ever made a personal commitment to Christ. When I was in eighth grade, I made the best and most important decision of my life. I gave my life to Jesus. One night after the service, during the revival that lasted a whole month at the Caney Pentecostal Holiness Church, I told Mom that I wanted to give my life to Christ. So, we kneeled and prayed right by her bed and I have been living for Christ ever since that night. It was the summer of salvation as my uncles, Mick and Sam with their wives at the time, Kim and Marla, all were saved and then my papa got saved during the revival. That was the best summer ever. We were all so fervent about serving God. My papa would pass away the next year and what a comfort to know that God had extended his grace and my papa was in heaven.

When in eighth grade, we started attending Midway church where Sam Vaughn was pastor. I became such close friends with my cousin, Shelly Watson Buttry. Shelly was my dad's first cousin. My dad was the oldest grandchild and Shelly was the youngest. Shelly was such an excellent role model. She was in her early 20s, but she always took time to make me feel special. Shelly led worship at Midway Church and I sang with her. Shelly had such a gentle heart and spirit and she nurtured the same in me. We would sit through church with my head laying on Shelly's shoulder. I remained close to Shelly throughout her life. She married Brad Buttry and moved to Lawton when I was a senior. I had a hard time forgiving Brad for stealing my role model, but he won me over and I soon saw what everyone else saw, they were made for each other. They were both musically talented and devoted to God. I went to see them occasionally while I was in college and they came to games that were near them.

I wrote the following paper as a school project in the 8th grade:

My role model

My role model was Shelly Watson. She was 20 years old and was my favorite cousin. She lives in Coleman and goes to school at Southeastern. Shelly was the sweetest person I know. She was also the one person who would do anything for me. If I were in trouble she would help me in any way. All I have to do was call her. That's why she my role model because she loves me so much. We have a lot of things in common. We both belong to the same family and go to the same church where she plays the piano and plays better than anyone I have ever heard. She sings really good too. Better than Whitney Houston.

Shelly was skinny, beautiful, and she's a lot of fun to be around. I would spend every day with her if I could. She helps me with my homework and beats me on the basketball court, but that's only because I let her.

She was a great example to me because she walks the straight and narrow in a world that doesn't. I love her a lot and I want to be just like her.

Okay, Shelly asked me to add the part about Whitney Houston but I really didn't mind.

She has a beautiful voice and taught herself to play the keyboard. Musical talent was strong in the Watson family. My dad played drums at church too. His cousins, Darla and Carla Watson, could also sing and play as well as Linda Watson. It was hard to beat family harmony.

Mom and Dad never made us go to church. We looked forward to and loved it. I told you about the month long revival we had at Caney and we never missed a night. I was always so excited to see what God was doing. There was nothing that compared to witnessing someone getting free from sin and receiving the love of God. So, church played a huge part in my life. Matt and I grew up in that Pentecostal Church; such great memories there with people who still seem like family. There are so many benefits of a small church. You become close. There were many church dinners with some of the best food ever at Caney Pentecostal Church with Linda Noak and Lucille Broughton. Darci Delay Justus, Matt and

I would often sing together on the stage at church. Darci's Mom, Darla sang and played piano. My dad played drums. Darci was the one with all the talent. I hope she still sings for God somewhere. Robin and Shelly Noak and Heather Broughton Milam were some of my favorite people in my early years. It is so nice to see them still serving God.

Later, I attended the Wednesday night youth services at Day Spring where Seth Swindall would be my youth pastor. I really liked going to church there. The next year, after I got my license, I started going to God's House full time while my brother and parents remained at Midway Church. It wasn't long before they started going with me to God's House because we wanted to worship together as a family. Darrin and Sheila Begley were the pastors and their impact on me was huge. They helped me find my identity in Christ. I always looked forward to church and was always gathering up a crowd to go with me. Even in college I would tell people about my church and bring them home to experience God with me. I attended Servant's Heart Church in Weatherford on the weekends that I couldn't come home. They were such nice people, but I still missed God's House. Darrin and Sheila saw something big in me long before I did. Pastor Darrin came to Midway to preach once when I was in ninth grade and he told me that I was called to be like Esther, of the bible, who was brave and God used her to set people free. He said that God would make me a witness to His people and that I would grow to be a great leader. Mom wrote this down in her journal and would remind God in her prayers, "God you have called her to do great things for You." The Begleys always inspired me. They always encouraged me. I love them for encouraging me and helping me find my identity in Christ, not in the things I was doing. Pastor Darrin would always say, "basketball is not who you are, it is what you do." Christ alone would define who I was.

My mom liked to walk when she prayed. At night, I could be in bed and hear her walking and talking to Jesus, proclaiming God's promises and coming to an agreement with the words that had been spoken over her children. My mom also taught me to worship. She always liked to have praise and worship music playing in our home or in the car. We had this game that we would play on long trips where we would put the radio on scan and see who could name song before it changed. We would keep score. My mom was horrible at the game because she only listened to gospel music and there were very few gospel stations. She would always say, "Who wants to be on my team?" and there would be absolute silence because we knew we would lose if she was on our team. She knew it too, but would act serious and then say, "Dad, you have to be on my team."

I loved to worship. I would be absorbed in the presence of God with my eyes shut, hands extended down, singing and praising God. It is like that now, except now I am in the very presence of our King.

During the summer of 2004, I went on a mission trip to Scotland. We were gone ten days. It seemed like forever to Mom because we didn't have contact. I had so much fun and loved it there. I am very thankful that I had the opportunity to go. One day, while in Scotland, we were having this conversation among friends about death and dying. I think it was because of Sean Hall's recent death and how much we wanted him to live. There was a discussion about how hard people prayed for Sean to be healed and raised because they wanted him to come back and I told Melissa Smith, "If I die don't pray to bring me back because I will be in heaven." I had that kind of confidence in my walk with God. There was no fear of death. The bible says, "To die is to gain." I believed that. We also went into town and I had fun dancing with the men in kilts. The experience was amazing and I could see myself doing more mission work.

BASKETBALL

"All athletes are disciplined in their training.
They do it to win a prize that will fade away, but we do it for
an eternal prize. So I run with purpose in every step. I am not
just shadowboxing. I discipline my body like an athlete, training
it to do what it should. Otherwise, I fear that after preaching
to others I myself might be disqualified."
(I Corinthians 9:25-27)

God was about to give me a platform to witness for him. He gave me basketball. He gave me the talent and I wanted to make sure I used it to glorify him. As I mentioned before, in eighth grade, I started to show some ability to play basketball. I moved to Tushka in ninth grade and began playing for Coach Kris Hall. I had not played high school basketball yet and these girls were big time players. Emily Rowton and Emily Eaves would go on to play at the college level. I had never even played high school ball and here I was with these great players. I was intimidated. I lacked confidence. Coach Hall was one of the best fundamental coaches around. He taught me so much about the game. Matt and I were both players with high basketball IQs because of him. He demanded excellence and used negative remarks to motivate. This method was not always effective with me. I already wanted to please the man, plus my parents were never negative so I was not used to this. Coach Hall was hard on me just as he was everyone else and I probably put a lot of pressure on myself. I don't think I was much help to the team even though our team was very successful. I was a starter as a freshman, but, as I said, I did not play with a lot of confidence. My mom would always pray for me and tell me I didn't have to play. She never pushed me into sports. She enjoyed watching me, but she would feel so bad for me if I played bad. She was always positive and even after my worst game she would find something I did well and focus on that. A lot of parents live vicariously through their child's sports, but not my mom. She was one of the parents who really wished their child didn't play because of all the pressure and hurt that it involved. We understood even then that God had given me the ability to play so that I could use it for the Kingdom. We prayed everyday on our way to school that God would give me the strength to endure. After Christmas break, I noticed a change in Coach's attitude toward me, he criticized less and was even starting to focus on some of my strengths. This helped to build my confidence and I scored seventeen points in a game against Mill Creek. During the playoffs in my freshman year, I was the leading scorer against a very good Battiest team. We made it to State my freshman year and won our first game. We lost in the semifinals to Cashion who was the eventual State Champion.

The summer between freshman and sophomore year I had a decision to make. There was a conflict between the Tushka team camp and church camp. I loved going to Darrin and Sheila's church camp and didn't want to miss. I was still scared that Coach would be really upset with me. I decided to pray about it and later got Greg Garison to talk to coach about it. Greg was the school counselor and a family friend. I always called him, "my counselor." He was also good friends with Coach Hall and agreed to mediate for me. Coach Hall gave me his blessing to go to church camp and miss team camp.

My sophomore year, Emily Eaves and I were the only ones left from the all star team. She had the highest vertical and could get nearly every rebound and would throw down court for me to get an easy lay up. We surprised a lot of people that year. We had a good season and made it to Area in the playoffs.

My junior year we were successful also with Stephanie Moore who was a great rebounder. We also had Ashley Gammon, Ashley Jones and Melissa Henry. We also made it to area tournament that year.

My senior year, my cousin Cassie moved to Tushka and we would play together for one last season. Cassie was an incredible talent. She was a complete player. She could dribble and break any pass anyone tried to throw at us. She could see court so well and make amazing passes. She could also shoot from anywhere and had such a quick release she was hard to guard. She could also take you off the bounce and with her quick hands played great defense. My senior year we made it to state playoffs and lost to my friends from Allen in a close game. It was great fun. Melissa Henry cried so much after our loss at state not because of our defeat but because she would miss playing with me. I knew exactly how it felt.

My parents never talked to Coach. They never interfered with him. We prayed for him and for me to handle it and grow from it. God answered. Maybe it was that I had gotten to know Coach and came to understand that he really just wanted me to get better and realized that this was his coaching style, so I didn't need to take it personally. Maybe it was that I started playing better and he didn't have as much reason to criticize me. Emily Eaves would be leaving for college and I really missed her, on and off the court. I had to step up my game without her there to help me.

I always tried to improve my game. Each summer, I would spend time in the gym adding some dimension that I was lacking. Emily Eaves was an excellent defender and I wanted to not only be able to shoot three pointers, I wanted to be able to take my defender off the bounce if they tried to get guard me too closely to defend "the three." I played one-on-one all summer with Emily and this helped me develop my ability to penetrate with either hand so that I would be more difficult to guard.

HOLY MOMENT

By my junior year of high school I would become one of the most potent offensive players in the state. This was back when there was a ton of talent in Oklahoma high schools. Class A was especially loaded. You had Stephanie McGhee of Howe and Jenna Pumley of Frontier, both signed with OU. There were numerous Class A players that would go on to play at the next level. Tushka opened the season at Calvin and I led scoring, with 29 points and 8 rebounds. Next up was Wapanucka and I had another impressive outing with 26 points and 4 rebounds. However, Coleman is where I set my personal career high of 40 points in one game. There was one problem, Boswell's coach was in the audience and he was making a plan to stop me at our game scheduled for that Friday night at Boswell. Boswell was a tough matchup for us anyway just because of their size, but they also had a great shooter in Marila Pebworth. Marila and I became great friends after meeting at a team camp the summer before. When we played Boswell, I saw my first ever "box and one defense" which was essentially designed to deny me the ball. They face-guarded me and kept a fresh player on me so I couldn't wear the defender down with my quickness. The "box and one defense" allowed that if I should touch the ball and get past my defender the rest of the Boswell's team was to immediately help guard me. It was designed to make someone besides me beat you. I worked so hard to get open, but couldn't even touch the ball. Going into the fourth quarter the score was Tushka 23 and Boswell 26. I was fouled with the game on the line. With only a few seconds remaining and Tushka down one point, I shot the free throws for the win. At this point, I had only scored 6 points the entire game. Boswell's coach called a time out to "ice the shooter."

After a quick huddle with Coach Hall, the team walked back onto the court where I called my own huddle and told the team "Let's pray I can hit these shots." I remember this moment vividly. My mom said it was like a holy moment as this holy hush fell all over the gym as everyone knew that I was praying with the team. Mom had always taught us that God was closely involved in every detail of our lives so if it was important to you, it was important to God. I knocked the free throws down and Tushka escaped with a 37-36 win. Just about every game after that, I would see that same "box and one defense," but with Coach Hall's help of having the team set screens for me, I would learn to master it. By regional tournament, we would again face Boswell and it was another epic battle. I had bronchitis and didn't feel well at all, but we only had seven players on the team. I couldn't sit out. At the end of first quarter, Tushka led 12-10 and 25-22 at the half. At the end of three, it was 29 to 26. I poured through 30 points for the 41 to 32 win. I was the only player on the team to score a field goal. I had mastered the "box and one defense!" The athletic director from SOSU found me after the game and said, "Get ready to be a savage." God blessed me so much and showed me so much favor as I dedicated my life and my talent to Him.

I loved Coach Hall. He expected a lot out of me because he knew I was capable. On the way home from SWOSU that last weekend, I had Mom to drop me off at the gym for Matt's practice so I could see Coach. I am glad I got to say goodbye to him. He was very important to me. I always prayed for him. My senior year, he asked me what I wanted for graduation and I told him that I wanted him to come to church with me. He kept his word and came. I was so happy.

At the sports banquet my senior year, he choked up when giving my awards and saying how much he would miss me. If you knew Coach, you knew that he didn't get choked up very often. I remember his words distinctly. He said, "When players leave, you start preparing yourself mentally and think of the things you are not going to miss about them, but I can't think of one bad thing about Kayla. She is simply the best kid I have ever coached." He was referring to my moral character, not my basketball skill. God gave me a platform and I wanted to be a good example and make sure that when kids looked up to me that they saw Jesus. I tried to live it. God called me to be a leader. I had the distinct honor of making both the McDonalds' All State team and Coaches' All State team along with numerous other awards. I went on to play for a great coach at SWOSU. Basketball was a huge part of my life, but I never let it define me. Basketball gave me a stage. My identity was in Christ alone.

I found Coach Hall's letter for the All State recommendation on his desk. It was so sweet I had to sneak a copy. His words about my character meant so much and the fact that he had such a high opinion of me made it worth all the negative things he had ever said. One of my favorite memories was him telling me he loved me after a game. That was so huge that I wrote about it in my journal that night. After my death, I had my mom copy that page from my journal and go by and lay on his desk at the gym. I knew he needed to know that I knew he loved me and I did.

Coach Hall's letter of recommendation for All-State.

Kayla has been a four year starter on teams that reached two state tournaments and two area tournaments while winning 96 games. Kayla scored 2.068 points in her career at Tushka despite that many times in the last three years she faced double and triple coverage. In one game, as a Junior (Regional Consolation Finals) she was the only player on our team to make a field goal in a winning effort. Several other times in her career she has outscored the opposite team by herself.

Kayla is a "coaches" player. She has been all about winning no matter what role I asked her to play. During the playoffs this year, every game we played Kayla guarded the best post player on the opposite team, doing an outstanding job every night out.

I don't think I have had one player in 13 years of coaching who I would rather have take a big shot than Kayla. Her practice habits are exceptional. At times during her career she shot over 200 three pointers a day, after practice.

Even though she is small and not very athletic, Kayla is being recruited by several universities and will have a chance to play at the next level.

As good a player as Kayla is, I personally feel she is a better person. I don't think I have ever coached a more honest, genuine, down to earth person. Kayla's selfless approach to the game and to life, in my mind, makes her as good a candidate for All-State as I have ever had.

We grew to respect each other so much. We were very close. I am so glad that I got to tell him goodbye. He would be one of the pall bearers at my funeral.

COLLEGE BASKETBALL

*"Whether you turn to the right or to the left, your ears will hear
a voice behind you, saying 'This was the way; Walk in it.'"*
(Isaiah 30:21)

I had narrowed my choices to SOSU in Durant which was 20
minutes away from home or to SWOSU in Weatherford, OK,
four hours away. Southeastern seemed the logical choice for a girl
like me who so enjoyed being close to my family and friends. Yet,
when I went for a visit at Southeastern, I just didn't click with the
team. I didn't fit in. Then I went to SWOSU and immediately felt
at home with Coach and the girls who shared my faith.

Coach Pond recruited high character players who would not
have problems off the court. Our team was extremely close and
it became a second family to me and the rest of the girls. Coach
Pond did a lot to encourage this off-court chemistry that would
enhance the team on the court. We went on camp-outs, we did
ropes courses, we were always getting together, and these things
made our team bond. Kayla Horn was someone I had admired
in high school. She played for Hydro and they had won two
state championships. She was a year older than me. We became
inseparable friends who were leaders on and off the court. We
were very vocal about our faith and understood our purpose.

We were not here just to play basketball. We were always having Bible studies with others in our dorm or with friends we had made. We carried our bibles everywhere just as a way to witness for what we stood for and what we were about. We went to Chi Alpha and Fellowship of Christian Athletes (FCA) and every Christian event we could find. We wanted to share our faith in every way possible. Kayla Horn and I didn't live together the first year, but I stayed at her room all the time. The second year, we were roommates. By the third year, we had moved into a house with Grace Ann and Stephanie Jones who were twin sisters who were also on the basketball team. Their brother, Matt Jones, had been a star quarterback at Arkansas and had been drafted by Jacksonville. He purchased a house for them and they let us live with them rent free. What a blessing. Of course, I would only have a few short months there before going home.

Coach Pond wrote this regarding my recruitment and athleticism:

I had only seen Kayla play on video prior to bringing her in official visit. What I saw on the video was impressive and I couldn't wait to see her in person. Kayla came for a visit in March and played pickup with the current team members. She was the best athlete in the gym. She was extremely quick and fast. She was very agile and she could shoot, not a bad combination for a guard. Kayla's athletic ability could be summed up in that she could jump out of the gym, she was super quick and a great shooter. She also had great court vision and could see the court so well. She knew when to push the pace and when to slow it down. These types of players didn't come along that often. She was so much fun to watch because you could tell without a doubt that she loved to play.

Even though I knew she was a great athlete, over the course of the two years she played at SWOSU she continued to impress me. She worked harder and more intensely than any other player that I had ever coached. I think the competitiveness in her drove her daily.

As much as her athleticism was a positive attribute to her as a player, her love of life and all people was something I had never seen before. She was truly an amazing young lady and I think about her daily and still miss her ornery little giggle.

Maybe Coach Pond liked to keep a professional distance, maybe it was just her personality, but although she loved her players she wasn't especially affectionate to her players. That was before I came. I not only wanted a hug every time I saw her, I insisted on telling her I loved her. Even when she was mad at the team and walking out the gym in frustration, I could be heard yelling, "I love you Coach Pond." It wore her down. The love and the laughter helped unite the team and our chemistry, both on and off the court, was exceptional. Many kids who have been superstars at the high school level had difficulty adjusting to the college game because of their egos. Just about every player on our team had been a superstar in high school which usually leads to conflicts and problems with team chemistry. SWOSU didn't seem to have this issue probably because of our love for each other and great coaching. I can't imagine a better college experience. I absolutely made the right decision to go there instead of staying at home and playing at SOSU.

I can't imagine a coach who would have been better to my parents after my death than Coach Pond. She made every effort to include them with the team. The first year after my death, Mom and Dad spent thanksgiving on the road with the team. They ate at Amber Hammock's house and stayed with the team as they played at Oral Roberts University. Also, Tushka had a night to remember me as one of their most decorated players and, of course, Coach Pond and the whole team traveled to be there with my family. Mom often went on road trips with the team. Coach Pond called her at least twice a week. Long after most would have forgotten, Coach continued her relationship with my family. You have to remember that they didn't really know Coach Pond other than to speak with her briefly at a few games. They had only heard of her through my stories. I never had one bad word to say about Coach Pond. She made me want to be a better player. In high school, I was accused of only liking to play on one end of the floor. I was not known for my defense. With Coach Pond's encouragement and teaching, I would become one of the best defenders on the team and often drew the assignment of guarding the best offensive player of the opposing team. Two years later on senior night they honored what would have been my last game. Mom, Dad and my brothers were in attendance and just moved to tears at the place that I loved so much and those who returned my love so overwhelmingly. The Ponds and my family are bonded together by their deep grief and shared love for me. They are so close, seven years later, they are considered family.

Some of my happiest moments playing basketball were at college. We had so much fun playing and on the road trips. A few weeks prior to the accident, I was at home lying on the couch with my head on Mom's lap, as we watched a WNBA game. Mom had always taught us to dream and believe that we could do anything. So, I asked her, "Mom, do you think that I would ever be good enough to play in the WNBA?" She looked at me and said, "They probably have people scouting you right now." I grinned and laid my head back in her lap. I always loved to play basketball, but it had served its purpose and was about to end.

While my family was driving to the hospital Mom called Kayla Horn to tell her about my death. Kayla Horn called Coach Pond and the rest of the team heard the news as they gathered at Kayla's house. They were in shock and disbelief at the news. Coach Pond was devastated. We had become very close. I had stopped by her office daily to check in with her and we had developed a mutual affection for each other. I don't think she ever recovered from it emotionally and resigned from coaching a few years later.

Coach Pond wrote me this letter after my death.

I Can't believe it has been four years since your accident. I think about you almost every day. You were such a great influence on me and everyone who knew you. I have a closer relationship with God for the example you provided and also what I have learned through your death. I know there are a lot of people who will see you again in heaven just because of you and the example you provided while you were here. You did leave a legacy here on earth. You lived for people to remember what you stood for and not what you accomplished. I thank God I was allowed to be a part of your life for even just a short while. I miss you and I know I will see you again

BOYFRIENDS

*"Flee from sexual immorality. Every other sin a person
commits was outside the body, but the sexually immoral person
sins against his own body. Or do you not know that your body
was a temple of the Holy Spirit within you, whom you have
from God? You are not your own, for you were bought
with a price. So glorify God in your body."*
(I Corinthians 6:18-20)

Although I had a cute figure with a skinny waist and a flat
stomach, I always dressed modestly. I never wore a bikini or
even belly shirts that would show a part of my stomach. My motto
was "If you will show it, you will share it." Once, while I was in
high school, I wore a certain pair of slacks and a guy told me my
butt looked nice. I never wore them again. I did not want guys to
be lusting after me. I would not tempt them in that way because
I wanted them to know from the start I was not compromising
about sexual purity no matter how long we dated. You know what,
no one ever tried with me. I think they knew that would be the
end of our relationship.

I had very high standards for anyone that I would consider
dating. I wanted someone who was as committed as I was to sexual
purity. God always honored this and sent me some great guys. I

am thankful for my relationship with each one of them. Some of them didn't last long, but their impact was huge. When I moved to Tushka, Emily Eaves and I hung out a lot. She introduced me to my first boyfriend, Sean Hall.

Mom always said that she knew it wouldn't last. We were just too young when we met, but it turns out that neither of us would have length of years nor live to comb gray hair. We were there for a season and I am thankful for the time we had together. We were perfect for each other, we went to the same youth group, we were both committed to God, we were both full of love, we had huge smiles and we always greeted others with a hug. Sean was so friendly. He had the best social skills. The kind of person you loved from the moment you met. We dated five months. He broke my heart, but in the most gentle way. We remained friends. Matt Phillips and I even double dated with his new girlfriend, Tabitha Meadows. I wanted to be mad at him for breaking my heart, but his personality just wouldn't allow you to stay mad. He was so charming. Sean was killed in a car accident the summer after we had graduated high school. It was tragic. The whole town mourned for him. We just couldn't believe that someone so full of life could be gone so quickly. His service was amazing with praise and worship, drama and dancing, just the way Sean lived and worshipped. I always said I hoped my service would be just like his.

Next, I dated Matt Phillips or Fat Millips (he was not fat at all, lol) as I like to call him just for fun. We met when he came to Midway Church with his mother, Rita Phillips. He was such a nice guy and fit every criterion to be my boyfriend. He had been raised in church and was committed in his walk with God. He was also athletic and gifted musically. He played so many instruments and helped fill the void in the music department at church after Shelly Watson married and moved away. Matt played and his mother, Rita sang. We started dating and he would be my best friend throughout high school. He was a gorgeous guy who was also highly intelligent and very athletic. He played both baseball and basketball at Rock Creek. That was what we mostly did. We went to each other's games, to church, or the movies. We hung out a lot with my cousin, Jennifer and her boyfriend at the time that was also from Rock Creek. Matt was also extremely intelligent. He scored thirty-three on his ACT. Thirty-six is perfect and he was the perfect guy. I was hard on him. I remember once when he had gone to Austin, Texas, for an academic tournament and he called me to tell me that the team, including him, had eaten at "Hooters." Now, he wasn't excited about telling me this because he knew I wouldn't approve, but he also knew that I demanded complete honesty and accountability in our relationship. He called while Mom and I were at a Christian bookstore in Sherman, Texas, to tell me. I didn't take it well. I told him, "You should have stayed on the bus." I would have gone hungry before I would go there to eat. We all knew that guys didn't go to hooters for their hot wings. There were several calls back and forth. I told Matt, "I'm sorry Matt, but you are just not the one I'm looking for." He was very upset and unable to even concentrate on the academic meet. I think I let him sweat it out a few days before he and Mom were finally able to convince me that I should forgive him. I did, but I wanted to make sure my boyfriend understood the uncompromising life I lived.

We dated all through high school. We would then make the hard decision to go our separate ways. Man, it was hard, but I was going to Weatherford to SWOSU to play basketball and he was going to OU to become Dr. Phillips. I was losing my best friend. I could always count on Matt. He was so devoted to me. We agreed to break up. After consulting with Pastor Darrin and Sheila, I promised Matt I wouldn't date for a year. We needed time for our hearts to heal and I didn't want him to have further pain of seeing or hearing of me being with someone else. I would keep my vow. Matt was free to date, but I don't believe he did. We had been broken up for over two years when my accident happened. He was so sweet to my family. He came by the house immediately and sat with my mom, holding her hand and remembering with her. My parents loved Matt and are so proud of him. Not surprisingly, he went on to become an ophthalmologist and married my friend, Chelsea. She is beautiful and they have three beautiful children. I am so happy for them. I will never forget Matt. Matt gave the most moving eulogy at the memorial service.

My last boyfriend and love of my life was Chance Begley. The name says it all. He needed someone to give him a chance. I was willing to take the chance that I could bring out the best in him. Chance was Pastor Darrin's son, but he had been born out of wedlock before Pastor Darrin became a Christian. He didn't get to know my pastor (his Dad) until he was about thirteen. Although he was my pastor's son, Chance had a rough start. He had not known Pastor Darrin and his natural mother had a situation that required her to give him to her friend, Dodie, who ended up dying in a car accident. Chance was actually raised by Dodie's sister, Marsha, and her husband at the time, Jeff Rector.

Chance had trust issues and attachment problems. He didn't have a close relationship Pastor Darrin and his family. I hoped to bridge that gap. I loved his family. I was especially fond of Darrin and Sheila Begley. Pastor Darrin tried to have a supportive connection with Chance, but their relationship was strained for years. Like Pastor Darrin, I saw the good in Chance and was willing to take the chance that I could help him become the man of God he was called to be. My parents were reluctant at first. We talked about it and I said, "Mom, I have always honored you and Dad and I have never done anything to embarrass or disrespect you, but I need you to just trust me on this one." They agreed to trust me.

Chance and I began hanging out after church camp the summer of my senior year. My initial attraction to him was probably because of who his dad was and I had always wanted to marry a preacher. For whatever reason, I soon fell in love with Chance and he was devoted to me. When we were together he was passionate about God. You couldn't be in relationship with me and not be. I believed in him. I believe that I helped to bring out the best in him. I saw the good in him, but trouble seemed to follow him. Mom told me about 3 weeks before my death, "Kayla, I like Chance, but I just think that God has better for you." I became very upset and said, "Mom, I would want to die if you didn't love Chance." She calmed me by telling me that she would love whoever I loved. He was driving me home in his pickup when the accident occurred. He didn't call my parents, but then how do you call and tell someone that their daughter is dead. Chance had been staying with my parents while I was away at college. He went home with his brother, Clifton, when he was released from the hospital. My dad was upset with Chance because that was how dads are. They want to protect their little girls and my dad was actually mad at himself, believing that if he had denied me dating Chance that I would still be alive. So, things were tense between my family and Chance after the accident, but the next day Mom got up and did what I would have wanted her to do. She went to Clifton's house where she found Chance who was so distraught. She got him and said, "Come home." He did. I had hoped they would grieve together.

I knew that anger was a stage, a step in grief that you go through before healing occurs. Chance didn't know how to grieve. He had always pushed his pain away. He reminds me so much of my brother, James in that way. He denied the pain. My parents saw this as him not loving me very much. They didn't understand when he began dating again so soon. My parents and brothers were so grieved that they could hardly make it through a day and it seemed like Chance had already moved on. Of course, that wasn't what happened. Mom talked with Pastor Darrin. They agreed that Chance would come and stay with him for a while. She went home and told Chance they needed time and space and that she wanted him to stay with his Dad for a little while. He agreed, but never showed up at Pastor Darrin's house. He would begin his nomadic lifestyle of living here and there and his downward spiral into drugs and alcohol to cover his pain. My mom's one regret in my death was how they handled things with Chance. She says that they should have kept him at our house and helped him through the grief process; maybe he could have avoided some of the pitfalls. Now, Chance is becoming the man that I believed him to be. He has a wonderful wife and two boys. Mom is so proud of him and I am too. He was proving me right. I knew he was worth the chance. He is blessed with his wife, Tamara who, like me and God, can see the good in him and brings out the good in him. Mom asked Tamara for her permission to share about Chance and me. She said, "I love reading about your beautiful daughter and am thankful for her influence in Chance's life." He has found someone else willing to take the chance. Chance also gave Mom permission to write about our life together. He said, "I think about Kayla Beth every day." I can't wait to see him again. He better be here in heaven with me someday.

SHEENA'S STORY

"A friend loves at all times,
and a brother was born for adversity."
(Proverbs 17:17)

MISSING YOU MORE THAN WORDS
The Story of an Unforgettable and Irreplaceable Friend

By: Sheena B. Smith
January 2013

INTRODUCTION

As I begin to put my story of Kayla in words, I cannot help but regret not doing so sooner. I have written more brief thoughts and stories about the role she played in my life, and practically "hoarded" bits and pieces of Kayla throughout the years. Of course I saved the obituary from her service, and found and saved multiple pictures of her, but I also saved phone conversations, instant messages, emails, cards, scriptures, and the writings produced in various forms by others. Kayla was a part of my life for approximately five years; five of the most impactful and precious years of which I will never let go. I am left saddened that she is gone and I did not have more time to spend with her; yet grateful for every minute that took place and hopeful I will see her again.

PART 1: How Kayla and I Met

One summer in high school, just prior to my sophomore year, I attended a church camp and developed a "crush" on one of the members of the worship band. As camp was coming to a close, I went up to the member, Matt Philips, and we exchanged phone numbers. For a somewhat short period of time following camp, Matt and I talked on the phone and computer. We met together in person a few times as well. My "crush" developed into a bigger crush and I really liked Matt. I thought he was very attractive, intelligent, and loved the fact that he played in a worship band and played sports. Thinking back, it was; however, very evident that I was "chasing" him and he didn't seem quite so interested. I believe I was too excited about the fact that he was talking to me to acknowledge this fact.

Things took a turn one evening when Matt called and told me that he was "seeing" another girl and basically implied that they were entering into an exclusive relationship. I was completely caught off guard and devastated. Always having been the determined individual that I am, I decided I was going to "win him over" and keep what was developing between the two of them from turning into something real. I asked a lot of questions to people that knew about this "Watson girl" that went to school at Tushka. I put a lot of effort into researching who this person was so that I could know more about the person that was chosen over me, and to become better prepared to stand in the way of their relationship.

I was determined to win Matt back. I began by attending Matt's state baseball game in Shawnee, Oklahoma where I made it a point to sit with his Mom, Rita Phillips. Kayla was not at the game. After leaving the game that evening, I realized that my presence had not compromised Matt and Kayla's relationship. He was always honest and upfront, but kind and straight to the point. He never tried to lead me on after establishing a relationship with Kayla, but was never "mean" about it either. He just left it as it was, simple as that.

I continued to try to keep in contact with Matt. One night I sent him an instant message from my computer. To my surprise, he did not write back; but Kayla did respond. I was so humiliated. I had no idea she was there with him reading my pathetic excuse of over-bearing compliments and poor attempts to make Matt like me more than he did her. Although I cannot remember the words I used when I wrote him, I will never forget what her response was. The message she sent to me said, "This is Kayla. I'm glad we share the same thoughts about what a great guy Matt was." Although thankful my face was covered by a computer, I felt awkward about what had just happened and somewhat confused about Kayla's response to my message. Surely she was speaking with sarcasm, boastfulness and pride. There had to be a significant amount of disgust and resentment towards some girl continuing to pursue her boyfriend—as nearly every high school girl would project when a guy was in the picture.

PART 2: Establishing a Friendship with Kayla

Further into my first conversation with Kayla online, I realized she was not "just like all the other high school girls." Although she might have been using some humor in her initial message,

47

it seemed as though she was trying to befriend me. We talked for a very long time that night on the computer; mostly about basketball. I was so confused, and for the next several months to come was not sure if what was developing into a friendship with "Matt's new girlfriend" was real or merely a game. I thought it to be possible that something artificial or with underlying components existed, of which I was unaware.

I was also very impressed by the amount of effort Kayla put into trying to get to know me. She went out of her way to exhibit kindness and was an influence in building my relationship closer to Jesus. The majority of the time, she was the one making the phone calls, emailing me first, and trying to find opportunities for the two of us to "meet up."

Kayla had a countless number of friends; friends that she had known better and longer; friends that she saw more often, and definitely friends who treated her better that I had. Even so, she made me, and most likely each of us, feel like we were her only friend in the world. I knew she did not "need" me in her life and she certainly wasn't desperate for me to be her friend. Despite these things, she still chose to be that person to me.

When there were holidays, even the smaller ones, I knew I would be hearing from Kayla. She would never give up on me and always made me feel important to her. I can recall a time in high school on Valentine's Day. I got to my car after school and turned my phone on; there was a text message from her telling me "Happy Valentine's Day" and that she loved me. I laughed, but was thinking about the amount of courage and thoughtfulness it takes for a friend to do something, even as simple as that. I did love Kayla but was not accustomed to saying that to others but she was very comfortable with sharing her love.

Over a short period of time, I was able to learn of Kayla's very spiritual side. She was without a doubt a child of God with an immense amount of faith and positive energy. It became evident that Kayla was very "popular," and for the right reasons. People, including myself and many others, looked up to her in a number of ways. Once I realized this person was really for real, she became not only a friend, but also a Spiritual mentor.

Kayla and I most often connected through church and sports. When we were juniors in high school, at a softball tournament at Tushka, I watched Kayla make an amazing drive-line catch and double-play. Although jealous of her athletic abilities much of the time, as our friendship evolved, I became more and more proud to be "Kayla's friend" and a friend of the "really good softball/basketball player (although this would come second to the other legacy she left behind as a person and Christian).

At the beginning of each new basketball season we would play Tushka as our first opponents. I can recall my basketball coach sitting us down prior to the Tushka game and telling me that I would be guarding "number 14." I was known for my quickness and defense, but in all honesty, Kayla "smoked" me and "stripped" the pride right out of me! The relationship between Kayla and I had strengthened by the time my senior year had arrived. During this first game, I tore a ligament in my shoulder that would later require surgery. With the amount of pain I endured, I cannot say that I have a lot of recollection of that night. I will say, however, that I clearly do remember Kayla approaching me after the game. She was mostly just saying hi, but she mentioned that her armpits "smelled like biscuits." I laughed so hard and will never forget that. She told me to smell them, but I gave her a "no way!"

I miss playing basketball with and against Kayla, even though she put my abilities to shame. I miss watching her play, and although I never told her, I would watch taped games of when we played against their team during high school to try to learn from her techniques. Watching Kayla make one 3-pointer after another at State was amazing. I also miss spending time with her at the softball fields and riding the four-wheeler with her there. Her athletic skills proved to be an instrument in carrying through with God's plan and an example to others.

PART 3: God's House and Kayla's Spiritual Impact

I had found salvation through Christ as a child, many years prior to Kayla and I meeting; however, I had never known a consistent, positive Christian role-model in my life until our paths crossed. I was not the person for God I should have been and still strive to be. Kayla's role-modeling, mentoring, and persistence in getting me to God's House changed my life drastically and opened my eyes to so much I had been missing.

I was a busy teenager, playing sports, showing animals, and taking part in a number of school functions and organizations. After spending most of my life as a "Sunday morning member" of my small home church, Kayla asked me to come to her church on Wednesdays, Sunday mornings, and Sunday evenings. This was a lot of church! I started by attending occasionally. I am not sure if it was because I felt obligated to because she invited me so much or not. I wanted to go, but I was so used to my routine and Wednesdays and Sundays were generally the only days I wasn't required to do something else outside of school hours. It was an inconvenience and long drive at first, but eventually paved the way for a great Spiritual journey for me and the blessing of a friend dearly missed in my life. Going to these church services became something in my life that I needed and even craved. During this time period one person even said (in a derogatory manner) that I was "obsessed with church." I took it as a compliment, and had

Kayla to thank for changing my routine into a new "spark" for Jesus.

When I first began attending Wednesday night services and noticed Matt Philips was in the worship band, I thought it would be very awkward, especially with me sitting next to Kayla. Kayla never paid any mind to it. She was confident in her relationship Matt; it just didn't seem to be a factor. We never had a conversation about it, but I made a commitment to myself, and for Kayla (without telling her) that I would never again try to pursue anything with Matt, and I never did. It was evident why he was so happy to have her in his life, and that was not something I wanted to mess with.

A great deal of my memories of Kayla took place at God's House. My favorite memory, and one that I think about often, was when I would walk into the youth/college worship building on Wednesday nights. Kayla would always save me a seat to the right side of her. It seemed as though she always knew the exact moment I would be walking through the back door (probably because she would be calling and texting me, making sure I was coming up until the point in which I arrived). She would be standing up from her chair, and sometimes praise and worship had already started. When I came in she would turn her head around and give me a huge smile, then point to the empty chair she had reserved next to her. I remember thinking, "There are so many friends she has here that she has known longer and that she was closer to than me, why would she save me a seat every time?" Even when I was no longer the "new" person she had originally invited to church, she still kept that seat open for me. At one evening service Kayla even brought me "Sweetarts" candy for no reason, other than her finding out that I really liked them. I was not accustomed to this kind of treatment by anyone, and had never had a comparable friend. I would stand next to Kayla while worshipping, and at times peek over at her because I loved to see the way she worshiped God with all of her heart. She was not "putting on a show." It was very powerful to see the connection she had with God and I wanted to find the depth of a spiritual relationship that she had established.

PART 4: College Years

Kayla and Matt (Phillips), although no longer a couple, had a conjoined graduation party at Kayla's house. It was a lot of fun, and bittersweet, as I knew things would never be the same once we each moved away to attend separate colleges.

Once Kayla and I started college in the fall of 2003, we continued to keep in touch, but we did not see one another near as often. There were occasional times I would be able to make it down to a service at God's House when she was also in the area for holidays or weekends. We talked on the phone often. She told me about her classes and basketball, and brought up her family most often. She would tell me how excited she was to get another brother (prior to James moving in with the Watson's) and give me updates on the adoption process. Given Kayla and Matt's apparent abilities, I remember asking her once about James' athletic abilities. In a very nice way, she expressed that yes, he was good at basketball, but that was not what really mattered, and she was not too happy about so many people focusing on that. Although Kayla later enjoyed playing basketball with Matt and James, and watching them play, she was mostly concerned about the fact that she was getting a new person in her life that she could accept and love.

As a freshman basketball player at Oklahoma Baptist University, my team was asked to complete a brief questionnaire relevant to each of us to print in "The Bison" campus newspaper. When asked about our greatest influence as a player, I put "Kayla Watson." I told Kayla about this and she was so excited. She often reminded me that I had not given her a copy of the paper yet, and a lot of time went by. I had always intended to give it to her; but unfortunately she was gone before she was ever able to see it. I passed it on to her parents following her death. It was a true statement. The person that "stole" the boy away from me would become a great influence and unforgettable friend to me.

In February of 2004, I became engaged to Chad Atteberry. We planned to be wed in July of that same year. We set a date (July 31st) and I had planned to ask Kayla to be in the wedding; however, God's House planned a mission trip that would take place during the same time. Kayla had already expressed her intentions of definitely being at my wedding, and I really wanted to go on that trip to Scotland. I considered many times changing the wedding date, but it seemed as though too much planning had been done, so we kept the date. I told Kayla to go to Scotland and not worry about it. I was very saddened that she could not be there and I could not go on the trip. Kayla had an amazing experience in Scotland, and I believe she did the right thing by going. I do, however, regret not going with them myself.

PART 5: Fishing Trip

The weekend prior to Kayla's death my dad took Chad and I on a fishing trip to Venice, Louisiana. The plan was to drive down and borrow a boat from one of my dad's friends that was in storage in Venice, and then take it out for a few days into the Mississippi River and further out into the ocean. It seemed to be a long trip from the very beginning. I sat in the back seat of the truck and was sleeping when at all possible. I remember Kayla and I texting as we were leaving the parking lot. I used to remember what we were talking about, but those details have left me. She and I used to joke around about who remembered whose birthday first (I was born on August 10th, and she was born on August 16th). I believe we were teasing each other about that. Once we finally arrived, we picked up the boat from storage loaded it with our supplies, then, went out into the marshy river that evening. We fished for a couple of days and I had not been catching as many fish as my dad and Chad, but no one had any idea about what would soon happen. I had never caught anything bigger than you could find in a pond, so when my line took off at a fast pace, strong enough to pull me over to the side of the boat, I knew we were in for something. It felt like catching something on the bottom of a pond or lake and thinking you had just caught "the big one," just to discover your line was only caught on something at the bottom, but this one was actually moving! Could I really have a fish this big on my line? It was a battle that took about 45 minutes. My arms were exhausted and I had very little energy left in me, even after some periods of help by the others. When we were able to finally drag the fish onto the boat, we saw that it was a redfish, just like the others, but much larger! The guide said that he had never before seen a redfish near that size that far up the river in the marshes. We took several pictures and I had the biggest smile on my face. After a very long couple of days, and a long day in itself with the rain and sun, it had finally paid off! Then the guide said that my fish would not be any good to eat, so he asked if we were ready to throw it back. Of course my dad looked at me and I was pouting because I wanted to keep it. He told the guide to just wait for a while so we could think it through. I had already decided I wanted it mounted, but I knew the cost was high and I wouldn't be able to pay for it, so I wasn't pushing it too hard. I was content at the time just knowing it was still in the boat with us.

When we made it back from our last fishing adventure, we laid out our catch prior to cleaning and took more pictures. The question came back up, "What are we going to do with the big one?" At this point the only options were to throw into the trash or mount it. We called around to several local taxidermists, but the price of a mount was ranging between $400.00 to almost $800.00. I must have had the saddest look on my face when my dad turned to me and said it was just going to cost too much. Then an idea came to me! I wondered what Kayla's Dad would charge, or even if he would mount an off-coast fish. I contacted Kayla and she found out for me. Ronnie agreed to mount it for $175.00. There was no question at that point . . . that fish was getting mounted! I was so happy.

I told Kayla we would be stopping by there on our way back. When we arrived we met Ronnie at his shop and Kayla walked up. We talked about spending time together sooner, but with me living in Stillwater we had not seen one another since I had moved that previous May. I remember her well that day. She had a special glow. There was something about her that stood out to me, but in a good way. We stood around, everyone talking for a period of time. Kayla said that she was about to leave to go to Weatherford (Annette later told me that she had planned to leave sooner but had waited for me without letting me know I was holding her back). As we departed, Kayla and I said our last good-byes. I still remember the smile on her face—the last one I would see in this lifetime, but had no idea. When we got back in the vehicle, my dad also mentioned that he noticed something "different" about Kayla—that same "glow" that I saw.

PART 6: Kayla's Death-Confronting the News

It was later in the evening on September 4, 2005, when I heard the heartbreaking news of Kayla's death. I was sitting at the table in my parent's home with my family gathered around. I watched headlights pull up the driveway and recognized them to be Chad's (my husband at the time) and his best friend, Sam. They had just returned from visiting his family in Tishomingo (we lived in Stillwater at the time, but were visiting that Labor Day weekend). He walked in with a horrified look on his face and walked up to me. He said, "Kayla's dead." We held one another and he cried with his head down. I was in complete and utter shock, but my facts were unclear. Chad had a sister named Cayla, and my initial thought was that she was the one that had died. It only seemed to make sense, given that Chad was the bearer of the news, had just come from his family's home, and appeared to be very upset. I sat there not knowing what to say or do, and once he was able to talk more he explained what had happened and that it was my friend, Kayla (Sam lived near Atoka and had heard from someone he knew at that time). With my mind switching from one tragedy to another, I stood up from my chair; so many thoughts racing through my mind, yet "drawing blanks" and in shock, all at the same time. I stated a few words about Kayla and how it happened to such a wonderful and impactful person. I resigned to my old bedroom and grieved for a long period of time. I had lost a good friend of mine when I was an elementary student, and it was very hard on me; however, I had never experienced anything like this and was not prepared for it.

After Kayla's death I became somewhat anxious about the more than 2-hour commute I was making each day to drive from Stillwater to Shawnee and back to attend college classes, play basketball, and work. I told Chad that I wanted to get a dorm room on-campus at Oklahoma Baptist University so I would not always have to make the late-night drive. I believe that having occasional time to myself in the dorms aided in the grieving process. I was able to have a lot of alone-time to sit and think, cry, and pray. I posted mementos of Kayla on the wall for healing and encouragement.

PART 7: The Memorial Service

I recall the morning of the service. While I was in Shawnee, getting ready in my dorm room, the television was on with news coverage about Hurricane Katrina in Louisiana. The sadness was overcoming and I was fighting tears back as I looked in the mirror and told myself to stop crying because I hadn't even made it to the service yet. I drove to Atoka, dreading passing through where the accident occurred. Upon arriving at the Atoka field house, I was overwhelmed by the amount of people present. I made my way up the bleachers and took a moderately high seat even with center-court. I looked down and saw Kayla lying there in an open casket. My heart fell as reality "sank in." I continued to look upon her family, Annette, Ronnie, Matt, and James, along with the many others. I could not fathom how they would be able to make it through. Annette says that God gave her the strength when she walked through the doors of the gymnasium. She knew God was there with her. I knew this too when I walked past the casket and offered my hugs and condolences to the family. Annette brought up "the fish" that brought me to see Kayla for the last time. She knew now how God had not only orchestrated that event, but so many more she would later share. God clearly paved the path and I believe it was because of Kayla's closeness to Him that He allowed so much to take place prior to the accident. Many of her closest friends were able to see her the weekend she died, and many things took place with Annette and Kayla that will forever be treasured by her mother. The words that were said and the time they shared that last week was such a blessing. These moments and memories have become a testimony of God's compassion for His people.

The service was profound, and I believe just the way Kayla would have wanted it. There was powerful worshiping and the presence of God was evident. Words were spoken by some of those who were very close to Kayla, such as her best friend in college, Kayla Horn-Hindman, Matt Phillips, and Pastor Darrin Begley. It was uplifting to hear their stories and memories. One thing that has never left my mind was when Pastor Begley made the statement that Kayla accomplished more for the Lord in her short life, than most people who live to grow old. This resonated a lot within me. It was so true; and made me evaluate my own life.

Summary: Kayla and Kayla's Impact

Following Kayla's death, Annette and I met for dinner. I had so many unanswered questions, and so much I wanted to say, but I knew it had not been long since everything had happened, and wanted to be sensitive towards Kayla's mother. It helped me to find some closure and begin the healing process. Annette was much more open, talking about Kayla and what happened than I had expected. Many of the things she shared with me will stay with me forever. She told me of a particular scripture that was helping her to cope. As it was passed on to me, it has helped me not only to deal with Kayla's death, but also to give to others who have lost loved ones along the way. The scripture was taken from Isaiah 57:1 (NIV), "*The righteous perish, and no one ponders it in*

*his heart; devout men are taken away, and no one understands that
the righteous are taken away to be spared from evil."*

Many changes took place in my life following Kayla's death.
People I knew at school had figured out something was going on
with me, and had begun to inquire about it. I explained that my
mentor and very good friend had died. I felt alone in dealing with
her death while at college, but spent a lot of time with God. Much
of the process involved taping copies of her eulogy, pictures, and
other memories to my notebooks I carried to class with me, and
hanging them on the walls. I created "Kayla" artwork, and tried
to write down memories of her and scripture that was given to
me at that time as I grieved. My favorite number went from being
22 to 14, which I wore on my jersey from that point forward.
Kayla's mother, Annette was a key person in the process. Her
faith, positive attitude, and openness were powerful. She hurt so
terribly, yet did not hide her pain behind closed doors. I think
we should all be more like this at times, and I believe it has been
therapeutic for her throughout the years.

I was later able to attend a ceremony that took place in Tushka,
which recognized her as a former student and athlete, and retired
her jersey. I obtained wristbands that read (wear 1 4 K). Although
I wore these daily in her memory, an even greater event occurred
involving the bands in Ethiopia when I took part in a missions
trip there the following summer. One of the first places my group
visited was one of Mother Teresa's "Mission of Charity" villages.
This particular village was reserved for the dying women and
children, most of them from AIDS, cancer, or other terminal
diseases. It was painful to bear and there was much sadness and
weeping. The children there could not speak English, but a certain
young girl was drawn to the wristbands I wore. She stood and
walked next to me for some time, clinging to the wristbands.
When I was preparing to leave, I felt like God wanted me to take

off one of wristbands (that I had not taken off in months) to give to this little child. As I slid it off for her, she smiled and my heart filled with joy to see that Kayla was still having a direct impact. I am not sure to this day why the wristband was so desired by this child. Most would ask for money, food, or clothing, but the band was all she wanted. She wore it proudly and my eyes filled with tears. I felt as though Kayla was right there with us.

Chad had no choice but to spend hours listening to me talk, cry, and weep as I attempted to deal with Kayla's death. At one point I even told him that I wanted to write a book about Kayla, but felt as though I did not have the insight to do so accurately, as a person closer to her could do. I was extremely saddened and desperate. I thought of Kayla as my closest spiritual mentor, and did not know how to go on without that and her in my life. I was fearful, but realized that she had prepared me in so many ways to use what she taught me (directly and indirectly) even after she was gone. It also made me realize the importance of accountability, friendship, love, mentoring, selflessness, and so much more.

Something that repeatedly circulated through my mind was that Kayla was in good hands . . . God's hands. With this being the case, it undoubtedly, yet unknowingly had to happen for a reason. Was it to take a person who God had found so much delight in, a girl that served Him wholeheartedly and completed her work on Earth, to preserve her from the suffering and pain humans endure? Was it to create a revival and renewing of souls left behind? Was it to make me a better person . . . for me to serve God with a stronger faith and show more love for others? If any part of what happened was because of me, I did not want to ignore what was in God's plans. For months, years, and even to this day, Kayla's life . . . and death has been a huge factor in my life, and always will be. I will never forget her, and neither will so many more people influenced by her.

Kayla loved church services, worship, and fellowship. God, friends, family, and her church family were everything to her. She put one hundred percent into everything she did, and she lived her life to the fullest. After having the opportunity to get to know her family more, I can easily understand why they were each so important to her and how she developed into the person she did.

It should not go without mentioning that had Matt not pushed me away for Kayla, I might have never met her. That time in my adolescence, when I felt as though my plans were falling apart, I had no idea that God's plan in my meeting Matt would be to connect me to Kayla and her family. So much of her life was evidence of how God works in the lives of His children. This has taught me the significance of faith . . . so that one day you can look back and say, "it all makes sense now." Sometimes we will never know why things happen the way they do, but nevertheless, we must keep focused on a greater being and a greater cause. As I recently heard on the radio, "Sometimes instead of asking 'why,' we should say, "Okay God, this was what the situation was, now what would you like me to do with it?"

I could write numerous additional pages about Kayla; however, some memories are to share, and others are to keep inside. I believe the theme of Kayla's life was clear and evident. She was and is irreplaceable; hundreds of us are eager to see her again when our time comes. She is missed, yet still here in so many ways. I am more than thankful to her and her family, and appreciative of others she brought into my life. I miss her friendship, her cards and calls, her smile, and her compassion, and her unique voice and wisdom.

I am so overjoyed that a portion of Kayla's life and legacy has been put into words by her very own mother. It was such a blessing that I will have a keepsake of her story, but also that everyone who knew her, knew of her, and even others who will learn of her will have the same. It is a gift to the world . . . to us all, and I believe our Lord was a great influence on what Annette and others have provided throughout this book. I am very grateful to Annette for allowing me to be a part of Kayla's story.

I cannot express the overwhelming appreciation I have that comes from having been a part of Kayla's life. Annette, you have become a friend, mentor, and inspiration to me. I also thank the rest of Kayla's family and friends for the support you have given towards the development of this narrative.

May Kayla's life continue to be a blessing and an inspiration to many generations to come. May they know Jesus and seek Him daily.

FAMILY

"As for me and my house, we will serve the Lord."
(Joshua 24:15)

I always loved coming home. I never went through a rebellious stage where I didn't appreciate my family. I was always happy to just hang out with "my fam." I loved to double date with Mom and Dad. I remember my home being filled with laughter, much of it at my dad's expense.

I loved to aggravate and my dad was my main target. He called it "driving him up" and I loved to do it. I liked to turn the heat up in the car until he was sweating and I would be dying laughing saying I was cold. Of course, I would have my vent closed which he didn't notice until he was sweating profusely. Another thing I liked to do was to mix up a combination of foods and stand there and beg him to drink or eat it until he would, just to get me to shut up. One particular time, I made him some chocolate milk which he doesn't even like. I kept saying Dad, "I made you a special drink, just taste it." "No Kayla." "Dad, just take a drink." "No Kayla." "Please Dad." I assured him that nothing was in it. He took a sip cautiously and it tasted okay so I convinced him to drink it all. He took a big gulp only to swallow something lumpy which turned out to be scrambled eggs left over from our morning breakfast. I continued to laugh about this for the rest of my life and always would ask him if he wanted some chocolate eggs. I liked to go to the grocery store and grab boxes of stuff that we already had too much of at home just to aggravate him. For instance, we would have ten boxes of cream cheese at home and I would gather ten more and throw in basket saying "We are getting low on this" or throw in stuff toaster strudels that we all knew wasn't going to be eaten. One of my favorite movies was "Hope Floats." I had a copy of it on both VHS and DVD. I would watch it often. Then it was on pay per view and I was like, "Dad, I am going rent that on pay per view." He said, "Kayla you own two copies of that," "But Dad, I haven't watched it on pay per view yet". He would say, "It's the same movie, I will put it in and you can watch it on video." I would reply, "But Dad, it might be different on pay per view." He would say, "Kayla I'm not paying $7.00 for you to watch a movie on pay per view that you already have on VHS and DVD." On and on we would go. When I went to college we would send each other cards. (Yes, Dad still has them.) We liked to see who could find the cheapest one. I thought I had him beat and was happy when I found a card for $0.49, but he beat me because he marked his name out and put mine and sent it back to me in a different envelope so he got the card for free. I bought him a tiny trophy for father's day that may have cost a dollar and then would re-gift to him each year. Our last father's day together, I bought him a red cap with this huge bill that I gave one dollar for, but I acted all serious about how nice it was and insisted he wear it out.

Oh, and I loved to steal his change. While I was generous with others, I was always very frugal with my money. I was always saving change and at one point had saved over $700 just in change. Dad wanted to keep his change. When he would come in from working for the day, I would say, "Dad, I hear change." He would say, "You are not getting my change." I would later get it so he started hiding it in different parts of the house from me. I would be so excited when I would discover his spot and wipe him out. I would exclaim, "Mom, I hit the jackpot, I found Dad's change." Oh, and then he would discover I had found it and he would start hiding elsewhere. It was a game between us. Oh, we had so many laughs in our home.

My parents never missed any of my games in high school and would travel often to see me play in high school. My parents were not usually vocal at games, but once when I was in high school I heard my dad yell, "C'mon Kayla" which was offensive to me because I didn't take games off. I was working hard against that "box and one defense." I told him after we got home from the game, "Dad, I heard you yell at me, I am mad and not going to talk to you anymore." He replied, "All I said was c'mon Kayla, I don't know how you pick that out of the crowd, but here is $20 will that get us back on speaking terms." I smiled and took the money. The very next game he did the same thing. I walked up to him after the game and didn't say a word just stuck out my hand. He knew what it meant and gave me another $20 while remarking, "You have literally broke me from yelling at you." Ha-ha and I did.

When he was around twelve years old, Matt bought a black Labrador retriever he named Opie. When he was about 16, someone gave him a chocolate lab named Molly. Both dogs were registered so Matt seized the opportunity to make money (that was so Matt). He sold the puppies and made about 2000 dollars. I wanted in on the action and bought a yellow lab named Daisy. Daisy became pregnant and Matt wanted me to pay him a stud fee for use of Opie (that was so Matt). I refused, saying, "Matt who charges their sister for dog service." Daisy was due to deliver soon when a neighbor ran over her leaving tire tracks right over her stomach and Daisy unable to walk. I was heart broke. Dad told me that the puppies are likely dead and Daisy needs be put to sleep. I said, "No, Dad. I prayed for those puppies, I believe they are going to live." Matt tells me, "That's just what happens. God couldn't bless you because you didn't pay me the stud fee." (That was so Matt). Miraculously, Daisy lived and gave birth to seven healthy puppies which I sold. A few weeks later Matt's dog, Molly, gave birth to her second litter and he planned again to line his pockets, but when he woke up the next morning and Molly had eaten all of her puppies I told him, "Matt that's what happens, God couldn't bless you because you tried to charge your sister a stud fee."

THE ACCIDENT

"Man's days are determined; you have decreed the number
of his months and have set limits he cannot exceed."
(Job 14:5)

A week before my accident I had been in "mommy mood" and wanted my mom to come stay with me at college so bad. She had such a demanding job at DHS and they didn't like to let her off, but God worked it out for us to get to spend that last week together. We had a wonderful time together doing nothing. She would call Dad and say we were having the best time and he would say "What are y'all doing?" and she would say, "Nothing." We visited my friends. We ate out at every place in Weatherford except for the barbeque place because when I eat barbeque I want it to be my dad's. What a wonderful week. My mom took me to class and picked me up. It was just like I was her little girl again and I told Mom this often. We lay on the bed, read books and watched movies. I just wanted Mom to be with me. It was a surreal time. Grace Anne, Steph, Kayla Horn, Jessica, and Tisha had gone to Dallas to watch the Cowboys play Jacksonville. They wanted me to go, but I wanted to stay with my mom. Mom and I drove my car home because gas prices were spiked that week.

I had a Mitsubishi Eclipse that I loved plus it got like 40 miles a gallon. Mom had driven the Explorer up and she left it for me.

I was excited to be home for the long weekend. I always enjoyed coming home. It was Labor Day weekend and Hurricane Katrina had hit. I wanted to go help. Mom said it would be impossible to get into the city and we should just pray. This prompted a conversation about heaven and gave my mom some things she would later look back on and see that God was giving her some words to comfort her. I told her "Mom I am so ready to go to heaven, this world's just too full of suffering." Then as she was sweeping and I was folding clothes I asked her, "Mom, will we know each other in heaven?" Mom responded, "The scripture says we will be known as we are known so I'm still going be your mommy in heaven." My friends from college came by on their way home from watching the Dallas Cowboys play. They spent the night. We all went to church the next day. My dad fixed my favorite food, barbeque. Mom made corn, fried okra, homemade macaroni and cheese, baked beans, and potato salad. All of my favorites and I thanked them profusely for the wonderful dinner. There was nothing like home-cooking after eating cafeteria food at college. After lunch, the girls went on back to Weatherford. I planned to stay until Monday because of the holiday but around two o'clock I said, "Mom will you be sad if I go home early?" Mom said, "No you go home when it is easier for you." So, I got ready to leave. I told Mom, "I think if I go home now, I won't be homesick anymore." Mom smiles and says, "Okay." Chance was going to drive me back in his truck. I always hated the drive back to Weatherford. It was so long and I would spend most of the time crying. I would sometimes make it to Oklahoma City where I would meet my friend, Brandon Drumm who would follow me. It seemed to help break up the drive. I was glad Chance would be driving me so I wouldn't be alone. First, we had to deliver a deer for my dad. Chance and I ran it to Durant then came back by the house to get my stuff. Dad had a customer at his taxidermy shop. I hugged Mom, told her I loved her and made her promise to "Come see me soon." She called Dad at the shop and said, "Kayla is about to leave," but the deer hunters kept talking so I didn't get to say goodbye to my dad. Dad later came in and asked Mom, "Is Kayla gone?" He said, "I keep trying to call her, but I had to leave a voicemail telling her to come back because she didn't say goodbye." They didn't know it, but I was already home. I had gone home early . . .

Around 4:30, Mom got a call from a friend, Carla, who lived next door to Chance's grandmother, Jeanie. Mom hadn't talked to Carla in months but there was no chit-chat, as Carla immediately asks, "Where was Kayla?" Mom said, "She was on her way back to college." Carla tells Mom, "Jeanie said there was an accident. She said Chance called his mother in London and that there was a bad wreck." There was no more information. They didn't know how bad the wreck was or where it had occurred. That was a very helpless feeling. Mom started screaming and saying "Let's go!" Dad, Matt, James and Mom jumped in the car and headed out. Initially, my dad who was big on details says, "We are not going anywhere until we know where she is." Mom says, "I know that she was headed to Weatherford, we will stop at every hospital until we find her." Mom started calling people to pray and to try to get information. She called Aunt Laura to pray and to help her in calling the hospitals in the area. Mom called Atoka Hospital, but they had no information. Just then Carla called Mom back to tell her that "They are at Valley View Hospital in Ada and she is in bad shape". Aunt Laura calls Valley View and they won't give her any information, but just said to get there quickly. When my family got to Tupelo near the scene of the accident, Aunt Laura calls my mom back. She said that she had called Valley View again and told them that they were driving at a dangerous speed and just needed to know something and the nurse said "DON'T HURRY" which meant I was gone. My dad was actually going over 100 miles an hour, but it seemed to be taking forever. As Mom hung up the phone she said, "Kayla is dead." Matt screamed, "Don't ever say that, and don't ever say my only sister is gone, she will always be alive in my heart." Mom was in some serious denial too, thinking there was no way that I was gone. Then her phone began blowing up with people asking if I had died while Mom was still trying to get information. Mom looked at Dad and said, "She didn't make it." Dad replied while choking back tears, "Yes, she did," referring to me making my true home in heaven. They didn't know about Chance, except that he wasn't seriously injured. They got to the hospital at 5:30p.m., and many people had already gathered. They were told by the nursing staff that I died instantly and I know that part of Mom's heart died right then. Life would never be the same. When I died, they also buried my future husband and their grandchildren that they wanted hold and tell them how much they looked like me and that Mom wanted to rock and remember when she held and rocked me. They buried my future wedding and my college graduation. Mom buried her best friend. They buried the perfect life that they knew and lived everyday. All the hope, joy, life and their very hearts died with me. As a parent you never think you can live without your children and the sad part is when you have to.

I was always a very safe person. I always wore my seat belt, but we were driving Chance's Ford Ranger and I couldn't sleep in it with seat belt on. Ever since I was little I would fall asleep in the car. In fact, during the period when I had my days and nights mixed up as an infant my parents would drive me around in the middle of the night to get me to go to sleep. I never lasted long in a car. I would do some of my best sleeping on the road.

At approximately 4:15p.m., Chance passed the Tupelo light and one mile and half later the accident occurred. What happened to cause it? We are really not sure and it doesn't really matter. Dad always wanted to know the details. Mom was able to let it go because she said that knowing how it happened doesn't make her miss me any less. The police report said that we were driving east on Highway 3 and driver (Chance) stated that he was run off the road by white Dodge pick-up that passed him. He first hit the ditch on south side of the road and then tried to get back on the road, but went across to north side of the road before truck overturn twice before ejecting me through the windshield because I was unrestrained. EMS received a call at 4:11 and they found me lying on the ground. My pupils were dilated and unresponsive. I had faint pulse as my body was shutting down but no blood pressure. Their efforts to revive me very pointless as I was already gone.

I officially died of a severe trauma injury to my head, I also had huge abrasions on my lower back and buttocks as well as a punctured left lung. I was an organ donor and parts of my skin, connective tissue and globes of my eyes were donated. Yes, Mom, my brown eyes are still shining. I did not suffer any pain at the end of my life. My spirit peeled from my body before it was broken and I was greeted by a host of overjoyed and excited witnesses as I entered heaven's gates.

My friends started to hear the news and the hospital was becoming full. People gathered at the hospital, at our house and at my granny Kathleen's house. Two of my closest friends recall hearing the news.

Robin Dale:

Definitely one of the hardest days of my life; I was in Frisco, Texas, picking up her dress to be my bridesmaid. I text her around 4:00 and she didn't reply . . . I was in the mall when Courtney called to tell me that Kayla had been in a wreck, but didn't know any of the details. We headed toward the car, but just when we were walking through the food court, Courtney called back to tell me she was gone. I couldn't hold my legs up underneath me. All I could do was sit on the floor of the mall telling God why she wasn't supposed to go yet. Still, to this day, I can't make myself say "died". It's still impossible to me. I love that girl so much and I know she would love to be a part of our lives, but I also know she wouldn't come back if she could. I hope I raise my kids to love Jesus the way she did.

Courtney Hill:

Cliff called Mom and said Kay and Chance had been in a wreck, but he didn't know any details. Mom and I were with my friend, Angie Nuttall getting a flat fixed at Dal-Fuel. I immediately started calling around and everyone had heard something a little different. So finally I called Matt Watson. He didn't answer, but he called back immediately. He said y'all were on your way to Ada. We got off the phone and a little later he called back, but he's just kind of silent on the phone. I was asking questions. He finally just spoke up and said "She's gone Court. She didn't make it". I honestly don't know what was said after that. It's so blurry to me. I came to the hospital. I don't remember much about being there either. I just remember that there were SO many people. I kept wondering how Kay could be gone and Chance not have a scratch on him. Now I look back and honestly think Kayla was too good for this world. Kayla deserved more than what this world had to offer. She witnessed to more in her short life than most preachers do in a lifetime.

My high school teammate, Emily Rowton recalls hearing the news:

Kay,

I'll never forget that day; that whole weekend really. I went to the OU game, then to Randi's to stay with her in Edmond. Then, I was going to Enid. I arrived in Enid about 6 or so and Natalie Mobbs called me. She told me that you'd had a wreck. I immediately called Coach. He confirmed that horrible news that I was just given. We both just sat there on the phone; not saying a word. We sat there for what seemed like forever, not saying anything, not knowing what to say. I burst into tears and we got off the phone. I cried for days. I moved to Enid in January for my job. As much as I like this town, it is still tainted for me because of that day.

Kayla Horn recalls hearing the news:

I remember I was driving in Weatherford. We had just gotten back to Weatherford and I was going to run some errands. Annette called me while I was driving. I remember driving straight to GNC because Mark was working. I threw the car in park and I was screaming and crying. I ran into GNC and tried to tell Mark as I was screaming. I just remember totally flipping out, like it couldn't be true. I remember the team coming to our house and everyone crying. I wanted to get back to Ada to pray and Kayla be raised from the dead because I thought her being dead just couldn't be true.

Kayla Horn then called Coach Pond and the rest of the team. They met at Kayla and the twin's home as they began to try to absorb the shock of my death. Coach Pond has been with my family every anniversary. They keep telling her that she doesn't have to come, but she always does. They are bonded together by their love and loss. It was no wonder I loved her so much.

THE HOSPITAL

There were so many people at the hospital. The halls were lined. My parents went in to view my body with Pastor Darrin Begley and Sheila, Pastor Jarod, as well as other church members who joined Aunt Laura, Mom, Dad and Matt. It just looked like I was asleep. I didn't have any visible injuries except for a small bruise on my cheek. Thankfully, Aunt Laura had cornered a nurse and said, "You've got to clean her up before they see her." She had seen me with all the blood. Aunt Laura had to be strong for my mom. She was not really my aunt but she was my mom's best friend and we are like family so I call her my aunt. After seeing me, she went into the bathroom, locked the door, and screamed and cried out to God. Then, she went and took care of business and stayed strong for Mom. She is like that. Mom says she has a gift for taking charge. I am thankful for the gift. My family needed her gift. Mom, Dad, and Matt were having a hard time when they viewed me and after a while Dad led them in prayer thanking God for the honor they had of being my family, praying for the grace to live without me and to release me back to heaven.

After finding out that I was an organ donor, Mom had to give information for my body. That took a while because they needed a complete health history for medical purposes. The lady asking the questions surely thought my mom was naïve, but it was true.

I had never used alcohol or drugs, I had never smoked a cigarette, I had never had sex. I was "pure" and proud of it.

My family got in the car to leave around 9 pm that Sunday night of the accident. Of course, the enemy, the accuser wanted to challenge my parent's faith. That was the trick he used when something bad happens. Can you continue to trust in the goodness of God? As the tears flowed freely, Mom settled the question as she said to my dad and Matt, "I won't question God, I won't ask why, I will trust Him that He knows best and someday it will all make perfect sense." This truth set the tone for how they would deal with grief. The only question they would ask God was "How can You use this to bring You glory." Even though their lives were shattered, their faith was steadfast always.

There was a crowd already gathered at granny Kathleen's house. Mom, Dad and Matt stopped there first to thank people before making it on to our house where more friends and family were gathered. For the next several days, our house would be full. The outpouring of food, flowers, gifts, and the steady flow of people was overwhelming. My family appreciated the love that was behind all of this kindness. Sue Ishmael, Dana Meadows, along with my aunts, Teresa and Myra Watson were there to take care of my family and greet people. They were like Job's friends; they would just sit in silence and let Mom cry. My mom would sit on my bed, hugging my pillow, sobbing "my little girl, my little girl" over and over. My mom's brothers also came to stay with them. They loved me and I adored them. Uncle Mick had never had kids and I was the first child in our family. They shared a special bond with me and I loved them. They were some of my biggest fans and never missed any of my games. I always wanted to make sure that they were in the audience because they would be encouraging me from the stands. Some people wanted to be left alone in their grief, but my mom was truly thankful to have the company. Sam stayed with them for a couple of months and it was so sweet to have him there with my mom. My Nan stayed with her for a few weeks too. My Nan was really sad because not only had she lost her beloved granddaughter, but she had to watch her little girl, my mom, suffer.

I don't know how, but at some point Mom and Dad must have gone to sleep the night of accident. Mom remembers awaking the next morning and Dad asking her, "Do you think we will make it? Losing a child causes a lot of divorces." Mom responded "We will make it. Who could ever understand the depth of the loss except you." Grief is always a lonely place; it means different things to different people. That is why we all grieve differently, our relationships are all different. The grief of losing a child is magnified by the fact that close family members that might be able to help in other situations are now dealing with the same grief. I am very proud that grief only cemented my parents' already strong commitment to each other. They could be eating a meal and tears just start rolling and they would not have to say a thing, they understood each other's grief. No one else would have been able to do that.

The next day, my dad had taken to the bed and said he didn't want to see anyone. Pastor Sam Vaughn came by and insisted on seeing him. Mom took him to the bedroom and he spoke words of comfort to Dad about how I stepped from this earth right into glory. Dad gained strength from his talk and prayer. He ministered to them. They asked him to assist our pastor, Darrin Begley in my service.

THE SERVICE

"For me to live was Christ and to die to gain,
I am torn between the two, I desire to depart
and be with Christ which was better by far."
(Philippians 1:21-24)

Pastor Darrin Begley really planned the service. He and R. Doug Lewis did an amazing job. Aunt Laura took my parents and Matt to both the funeral home and to Pastor Darrin's office to plan for the service. My family was just in no shape to think. Mom just sat there and said, "I should be planning a wedding," and Pastor Darrin said "She is now the bride of Christ." Mom told him how much I like Sean Hall's funeral and to make the service similar to his. I thought my service turned out perfect except the obituary didn't mention that I had attended school at Stringtown and I regretted this because that was where I found my first sense of belonging which was so important in my life.

Dad and Mom were standing in front of a packed gym. It was Wednesday at 11:00a.m., which means most had to miss class or work to attend. SWOSU brought a bus for four-hour trip that carried not only the team, but the student body. As he looked at crowd Dad said to Mom, "Remember when our little girl didn't have any friends, look at her now."

There were so many of my friends in attendance. I loved how at my memorial service we threw out social customs of a traditional funeral and just had church. I think funerals should do two things: they should memorialize your loved one and they should comfort. This was a comforting service. Everyone left uplifted and felt that they had been in a good church service. Brother Sam Vaughn eloquently explained to those who were shocked by the nontraditional service that this was how I lived, and this was my day; when you die you get to do it your way. That was so funny. If you knew me well at all you knew I loved to worship.

My dad had to help my granny in so he walked with her. Mom grabbed my brothers, Matt and James, and walked in with them. She didn't know it, but that was the way we had it planned. See, people needed to see that James was a son too and that he was loved and a part of our family. God was even in this small detail and it spoke volumes about James' place in this family. My mom sees my SWOSU team there as honorary pallbearers and she pauses to give them my "I love you" sign.

Oh yeah, my mom got to meet my friend, Irving Roland. I loved Irv. We shared the same faith. He played for the men's team at SWOSU and was a Christian like me. He had graduated the year before and moved to Boston to work for the Celtics. Irv and I had played phone tag over the weekend before my death. I had often told my mom about Irv, but she had never met him and didn't expect him there. She had seen him play basketball though so knew who he was. I was so happy when she saw him walking past my casket and she basically stopped the funeral procession to introduce herself. He and my mom became so close. He helped her through the grief. I usually called and text my mom several times a day and I never went to bed without calling and telling her goodnight. She missed my calls. After my death when the phone would ring late at night, she would automatically think it was me calling, but I was no longer just a phone call away. Irv found out about how I used to call her and being such a sweetheart he started calling my mom for me every night. They would talk forever. He was a busy man as he was now working for the New Orleans Hornets, but he never missed calling every night for the first two years. He helped her a lot with James, too. I so love Irv for taking care of my mom. He was part of the family now.

At my memorial service, the praise and worship was amazing and uplifting. It was special to be able to see my parents lift their hands and worship during the service. I have always loved to hear my cousin, Emily Lansdale Fincher, sing and she sang one of my favorite songs, "Running After You." They also sang, "Here I am to Worship" and "No Sweeter Name." The youth group from God's House performed a drama to the song "Total Eclipse of the Heart," showing how sin starts small but eventually destroys a person's life. It was amazing. I was so proud of them.

Brother Sam Vaughn spoke about being a parent and not being able to rest until you know your kids are safe at home at night. He said, "Ronnie she is safe at home, you can rest now, she is safe at home." He also said that at times like these you have to remember the givens, the absolutes. "Heaven is real. Kayla is there and we will spend eternity with her."

Pastor Darrin did a great job speaking about me and how important my relationship to Christ was. He talked about my love for my family including my brothers, Matt and James. James is African-American and had been adopted a year and a half before my death. While some in our community and family were reluctant to accept him because of his racial difference, it never bothered me. I loved and accepted him from the start. I would get so frustrated that the adoption process was taking so long and I told everyone about my new little brother. It was hard to imagine him as my little brother as he was very tall and would grow to be

6'8. I was glad that my death had helped people see past his skin color and bring healing to racism. Pastor Darrin talked about my love for all my family and how proud I always was to say, "Yes, Pig, Frog, Slick and Fudin are my uncles." I loved them all. He also mentioned my love for my favorite cousin, Cassie. Yes, we had experienced some difficult times, but we were really like siblings. We were only five days apart. I had loved Cassie since our birth. God had worked it out to where we got to spend our last year together at Tushka. We played ball together and had become close again. We had stayed in touch during college and I was sharing my faith with her. I had a bible for her, but I couldn't get together with her to give it to her so I left it at her parent's store just a couple of days before my death. It would be my way of continuing to reach her beyond the grave. She was so special to me. I was so honored when she chose to name my niece, Ryleigh Kay after me. My other cousin, Jennifer would also name her daughter after me, Harley Beth. They are both great moms and I love those nieces. No one could ever make me laugh like Jennifer could. We never got together that we didn't laugh endlessly. My journal was full of times that we shared together. Jennifer and Cassie were both great athletes too and if we had all stayed at the same school, we would have surely contended for some state championships. We did get to play a summer of AAU basketball together and had so much fun.

At my service, Daniel Argo shared a poem he had written and Chance shared a few words, but Matt Phillips would give the most moving eulogy of the day. Here is a copy of his words:

Hello friends and family, for those of you who don't know who I am, my name is Matt Phillips and there was a time in my life when Kayla was the closest person to me in the whole world. We went through a lot together and although our paths had diverged of late due to the different directions that God had taken us, I know that I can honestly say, as well as many of us gathered here today could, that my life would not be what it is today were it not for Kayla Watson. Kayla was a very, very special girl who it is not really stretching it much to say, "Did no wrong." If there was one word that I could use to describe Kayla it would be the word "pure." I looked up the word in the Webster's dictionary and it says, clean, clear, unmixed, spotless; genuine, sincere. Kayla definitely embodied all these characteristics. She loved the God she is present with right now as I speak above all else, and she had very absolute moral convictions that she would not budge on, no matter how easy it could have been for her to do so. She didn't trust or love easily, but when she did, she did so deeply.

One of the things I remember most about Kay was that she would not stand for dishonesty, not even a little bit. She always told the truth, and she required those close to her do so as well . . . at least if they wanted to stay close to her. She also always cared about others. I was telling Annette the other day that I remember the time back when I had first gotten my driver's license and Kayla was looking at it and noticed that I hadn't checked the "organ donor" box. She couldn't believe that I could be so thoughtless toward others. A few months later, my wallet was stolen and needless to say, my license still has the "organ donor" box checked on it to this day. The things she cared about most in others, however, were that they come to know Jesus in the way she did. Some of the times I saw her most excited were when someone she knew who wasn't saved came to know Christ.

She was also one of the most competitive people I ever met. Some of the biggest fights we ever had were over things like putt-putt golf. Another thing about her was she loved some of the funniest things and there wasn't a "girly" bone in her body. In fact, one time I bought her a bottle of perfume for her birthday, but the only reason I got it was that she loved things that were like miniatures of big things or oversized versions of little things, and the perfume came with this little locker that was about a foot tall that you could put stuff in. She loved the locker and I'm not really sure that she ever wore the perfume.

She was a naturally pretty girl of course, but unlike so many other girls, that was never an issue of identity for her. Most of the time, she would just throw her hair up in a little ponytail sort of on top of her head, but also sort of off to the side a little bit: the "busted bale of hay," as Ronnie used to call it. I remember Annette would always have to fight her to fix her hair and usually about 15 minutes down the road, she would look over say, "Do you care if I put my hair up in a ponytail?"

So many people looked up to her because she just didn't seem to care what other people thought of her. She knew who she was, and that's all that mattered. She lived a life above reproach; she was definitely of "in the world but not of it." One of the words that really jumped out at me when I read the definition of "pure" was unmixed." Kayla was absolutely unmixed. She didn't allow anybody else's opinion of right and wrong or what "wasn't really that bad" to alter the way she did things. She wouldn't even allow herself to be around situations where moral compromising was going on. I remember having to leave a room and go somewhere else many times because Kayla just didn't want to be around people who weren't acting right and it wasn't because she thought she was better than anybody else; it was just that she didn't want to allow "mixture" in her life.

The other word from the definition that really caught my eye was "genuine." She was the same person no matter where she was, and if her armpits were sweating really badly, or her stomach was in disrepair, she would always let you know. She didn't put up a front for anybody and she didn't try to hide anything. She was someone you could just be honest and yourself around.

If there were one thing that I could say to her today, it would be "Thank you for all the ways you have changed my life. I am the person I am today with the relationship with God that I have today in great part because of the influence she had on my life and the relationships that she brought into my life. She never compromised and she always pushed me and everyone else around her to do what was right in the sight of God. I regret that our friendship had grown somewhat distant recently but I will never forget the impact she had on my life during the time when we were the closest. She was an amazing, amazing girl and though her life may have been short, she lived it to the fullest and touched more people in a short time here than most that lived to be a hundred could ever dream of. I could never thank her enough for what she meant to me and my family. It has been an honor to get to share a little bit about her with you all today. Thank you.

My best friend from college who was also my roommate and my teammate gave a short eulogy. It was very sweet. Kayla and her husband, Mark Burns and his sister, Tisha, all moved to Atoka to go to my church, God's House. Grace Ann and her husband, Brady, also moved here and attend God's House. That makes me so proud. They were hungry for what I had grown to love at church. They just wanted to experience God. Kayla Horn told my mom once, "We were Christians before Kayla came; she just showed us how to enjoy it and how to live it."

Some of my other friends shared these memories from the service:

Amanda Gabbart:

I remember seeing girls from just about every team Kayla had ever played against. The service was truly a celebration and I have never felt a sweeter spirit. I'm convinced it was a glimpse of how worship will be in Heaven.

Melissa Isom Brazil:

I remember during Kay's service seeing you raise your hands and praising God like thanking him for her life here with you. I remember wondering how you found it in you to do that. It was the most amazing service I had ever seen.

Marilla Miller:

My favorite thing that was said, and still is true today whenever any loved one passes, is, "Heaven became a lot more valuable this afternoon."

Sheena Smith:

One thing I remembered was when someone (maybe Pastor Begley) said that Kayla had accomplished more in the 21 years of life (referring to sharing and modeling her faith and serving Jesus) than most people do in a lifetime when they live to be much older. I was also moved by the praise and worship aspect of the service. She would have wanted it that way. I saw the way God gave you and your family the strength to get through and how you felt His presence when you walked in. When I walked by where she lay, you were even were able to smile with tear filled eyes and mentioned how I got to see her because of the fish! I could see the strength in your entire family as you held one another. So many people and so much truth were spoken that day! So many lives impacted by her life.

Stephanie Miller:

I can remember all of us Stringtown girls wearing blue and gold ribbons in her memory I had to work and was late for the service when I got there I went to the gym floor and stood by Kim Swindall I can remember the songs and the drama and the words and memories but one thing stuck with me and it was the song I Can Only Imagine. It touched me in a way I hadn't felt in a long time I rededicated my life that day and it was because of Kayla.

MEMORIAL SERVICE AT SWOSU

In addition to bringing students by bus to Atoka which was a four hour drive, SWOSU had their own memorial service to help give students closure. Mom and Dad attended and wept openly at the beautiful tribute to their daughter. I had truly impacted a campus. There was a slide show of me, and Jason Barr, the FCA leader, spoke. He said although many knew me from basketball and how I loved to play, but my legacy was my faith and I shared it openly and freely. He told how I would go to the cafeteria and find someone who was sitting alone and start building a friendship and sharing my faith. He talked about how I always carried my Bible with me just so I could let people know I was a Christian. He said, just look at this packed gym and who would have thought that this little girl from an obscure town of Tushka in Southeast Oklahoma could have touched so many lives. What a beautiful service. Thank you, SWOSU and thank you, Coach Pond.

I had always been drawn to outcasts because I had been one. God used that experience to make me sensitive to others. I met Darlene one day in the computer lab. Darlene was older and was going back to school. I would often give her a ride home because she lived about 7-8 blocks from the school and she was really overweight. I would also meet her in the library and help her type up her papers because Darlene was not real techy. Mom met

Darlene at the SWOSU memorial service and just wept as they hugged. Mom thought most people would have walked right on by this lady, but those were the ones I was drawn to the most. She said I saw the beauty that God could see in each of us.

After I left, Grace, Stefanie, and Kayla Horn all started pitching in when they would see Darlene around campus. She would invite them into her house and they would sit and visit with her and pet her cats.

IN MEMORY

The university did several things to honor my memory including making T-shirts with my initials and number on them. Our gym where we played was called Rankin Field House and they sold Rankin' rowdy T-shirts with my number 14 and initials KW on them. They said my untimely death had affected the entire student body. One of my instructors also came up with the idea of making wrist bracelets for me that said "wear14Kayla." They sold them for my scholarship fund, too.

Our College newspaper did a profile interview with me during my sophomore year at SWOSU at the time I was averaging 9 points and 4 points a game and had started every game my sophomore year. I was second in 3 point percentage and in three pointers made. I had a three pointer in each of the last six games, the longest streak on the team. They ask who my favorite music/band was and I said Christian music and Third Day. My favorite food was barbeque of course. My favorite movie, my dad would know this, Hope Floats. My favorite TV show was "Boy Meets World." Would I read a book or play a PS2. PS2 was the answer, but actually the old Nintendo with Mario as my favorite game. We would stay up all night playing that game. Who was the biggest inspiration in my life? My mom. She has been my biggest supporter. I know if I quit basketball today, she would support my decision. Whenever I have a bad game, she is always there to encourage me. I can count on her for anything. How has basketball changed my life? Well, first of all, I had to come to Weatherford. Its 4 hours from home. I had to meet new people and make new friends. Second was just being a college athlete makes people look up to you. I want to set a good example for them to follow. What goals did I have for our team? I think we can beat any team we play. I think we will do well in Regionals. I have a lot of faith in this team. We could go far in the playoffs.

Kayla's family sitting: Ronnie, charisma,
Annette (grand-daughter, Kayden on lap) James.
Standing daughter in law, Monise and son, Matt.

Kayla age two with those big brown eyes

High school best friends, Kayla, Courtney Hill,
Alyssha Cox, and Robin Dale

Kayla and beloved brother, Matt

Kayla and Matt

Homecoming queen and Matt who was freshman at the time

**Tushka
basketball picture**

**Southwestern
basketball picture.
Always #14**

Kayla and Chance

Kayla a few weeks before her death

MOMMA'S BROKEN HEART

"He heals the brokenhearted and binds up their wounds."
(Psalm 147:3)

Three weeks after the funeral, Mom and Dad were scheduled to go to Guthrie, Oklahoma for an adoption retreat. They needed this break. They were going to go, but kids were not allowed so they left Matt and James at home and headed out. They got to Atoka and Mom said, "I can't leave Matt, let's go back." She called and cancelled the adoption retreat. I am glad they listened to God because they found Matt broken—hearted at my grave. They took him and went to Oklahoma City, just to spend some time with him. This was a crucial call because it gave them time alone and an opportunity for Matt to share his heart with them. It gave them time as a family to mourn. As they were leaving, Dad told Mom to buckle her seatbelt and she said, "Why, I want to die anyway," not thinking about how this must have made Matt feel. Matt said, "I guess it is hard, Mom, deciding which kid you want to be with." Mom immediately recognized her mistake and assured him, "God says to stay here. He could have easily taken us both when I drove us home from college, but He waited for another few days. God wanted me here with you and I would be just as heartbroken without you." Matt, our gift from God. The most comforting words ever spoken to Mom were from our gift from God. As they were preparing to leave for the service, they had a few moments alone. He seemed to read her mind as she sat quietly on the bed. He said, "Mom, you never did anything wrong, you were perfect." Mom said, "I know that was not true but thank you for saying that because if you think so, maybe she did too."

A few weeks later, Mom got the call that my death certificate was ready. She had to have it. She left work and drove to Brown's Funeral Home and sat in the parking lot for about two hours, crying. She couldn't make herself get out the car. It was a simple piece of paper but it was so hard because it meant "it" was official. I was gone. Then God whispered to my mom through her pain, "No, she is more alive than she has ever been."

THE VALLEY OF THE SHADOW OF DEATH

P salm 23 talks about walking through the valley of the shadow of death. I always thought it referred to a person dying, but realized it was for those who are left behind in grief to walk through the valley of the shadow of death.

Thankfully, my parents had many people who helped them in their walk through the Valley. My mom's best friend from high school whom I call Aunt Dana (Meadows) was there immediately as were other friends from school such as Sue Ishmael and Cindy Hunter. There were lots of times like Job's friends where they would just sit in silence because the grief was beyond words. Rhonda White and her husband, Jody, who had lost both of their children became close to my parents. Rhonda was such a generous and caring lady. I can't imagine losing both kids. Mom still had Matt, who was 17 and they had James whom we had adopted a year and half before who needed Mom so much. He was nearly 16 and had a lot of issues. I used to think God put him in our lives because he needed a family, but later realized Mom needed James as well. She was constantly helping him with school, keeping him out of trouble and traveling to watch his games. He gave her purpose. Matt and Mom have always been very close, but he didn't have issues and he had Dad who spent a lot of time with him in the woods. Plus, he had his girlfriend, Monise Watson, who helped him so much. James needed Mom more. Of course, she would be there for Matt too, but James was the one who made her focus on something besides losing me.

James treated my mom badly. He had issues with trust because his biological mother had abandoned him. He rejected my mom's love over and over for years. When I was there, it didn't bother her much. In fact, I remember one day being in the kitchen and James had rebuffed her attempt to show him some kindness and I said to her, "Mom, he doesn't like you." She said, "I know." I hugged her and said, "Don't worry, I love you enough for the both of us." That was how it was when I was there. I met that emotional need for Mom, but then I left and the wound came. James would hurt Mom so much, just when she needed him to be supportive and give her time to mourn. One thing James can never say is that he never had anyone to love him through the pain. She did. She would sit at my grave and beg God to release her from the pain of loving him. God would never do it because He knew in the end that they would share something beautiful. I am thankful God gave James to my family. What a beautiful picture of God's love for us. We continue to reject all that He offers yet He continues to pour His love out to us.

James never cried at my death. He avoided the pain. He sat through my service and never shed a tear. He was so out of touch with every emotion except anger that it would be years before he was able to cry about my death. He told Mom, "I wanted to, but I couldn't." Several years later, when giving a speech for his college class about someone who had influenced his life, he chose to talk about me. He broke down and cried and instead of being embarrassed about this he couldn't wait to call and tell Mom about this breakthrough.

Slowly, the initial stage of shock and numbness was wearing off and the reality of my death had hit them and my family started to fall apart, but I knew how strong their faith was and I knew they would make it. I am proud of them. This was a hard blow. My family loved me.

The first year of grief my mom spent in fear. Fear that she would never emerge from the emotional fog and that she would never think clearly again. Fear that she would never experience joy again. Fear that she would fail her remaining children. Fear that she would forget me or that others would forget me making my life meaningless. Fear of how to live without me. Fear of losing another child. This was what happened with James. Because of the fear, Mom developed an unhealthy soul tie with him. She was terrified he would leave her to go live with his biological family and she would have to bear the pain of losing another child. James learned to manipulate this fear and it would be years before she got completely free of this spirit of fear. When she finally did, it completely changed her relationship with James. She didn't have the wound anymore and no longer expected him to meet the emotional need that I did.

My mom started to journal her feelings about the loss of her beloved daughter. She started writing me letters to help her process her emotions. She was really struggling. We were so close. I cannot remember a time in my life when I fought with my mom. There was never a time when I didn't want to be with her. I didn't have "teenage rebellion." I was always so happy to see her and she would do anything for me. If I wanted to go to IHOP at midnight she would go. I would call her and say, "Mom, I am coming home, get us some movies, hot chocolate and a jigsaw. Let's stay up all night," and we would. I remember once when I was in high school she came into my room and gave me a book that she had just read, called "A Walk to Remember." She said, "You should read this, I think you will like it." I said, "Mom read it to me," so we sat up all night as she read the book aloud to me the book that she had just finished. That was how we were; we loved being together always. I think the hardest thing about my leaving was that she did not have anyone else as close to her as me. I was her only daughter. I had left her alone with a house full of boys. She loved them, but boys are different. They didn't share their lives like I did. They didn't want to go to the movies, work jigsaw puzzles or text her throughout the day with little tidbits of what was going on in their life. She missed taking care of me and mostly she missed sharing my life.

Here are some notes from my mom's grief journal:

Sometimes when I can't pray I just worship. Worship takes me into the presence of God and brings healing and comfort. Even His name was a prayer. Sometimes all I can say was His name.

Physically I feel so tired and exhausted but afraid to sleep because when I am alone in the dark, the death is too real. I can only pray that I will have dreams of you. Waking in the morning was the most horrible time because my first thought was that you are gone and I have to live another day without you. I only look forward to my death and to be with my baby again.

Emotionally, I just pretend that you are off at college. Denial, that was my main defense mechanism.

Your grave has become the most peaceful place on earth to me. A cemetery was no longer a scary place to me. It was so quiet and uninterrupted. I like to go there and pray.

I feel more hopeful when I . . . Matt and James are really the only reason I want to live. I don't think that they need me but I need to stay here and pray for them. I need to make sure that we are all together in heaven someday.

Grief makes me hypersensitive. I am offended at the slightest thing. Normally, I am not easily offended but now I get my feelings hurt when I think someone has forgotten you or that that they don't care about our loss. I hope I can get over this because I realize that this was really opening the door for the enemy allowing him to silently enter and create an offense that will lead to stronghold if I don't recognize and forgive. I know I must guard my heart. I get angry when I hear someone talk about how hard your death has been on Chance. Chance had only known you a year and a half the same as your brother, James. There was no way you can compare the grief that Matt and James experienced because Matt had a closer, longer relationship with you. The deeper the love, the harder the pain. I had nurtured and loved you from birth. Without love there would be no grief. I ask would I be willing to exchange my grief for never having known you? Is the love and the happy memories we shared worth the pain of losing you? No way. I will bear the pain of the experience of having gotten to love you and be your Mom.

I am really happy that Mom was relying on God's word. When she was feeling really down she would ask God to show her some promise in His word for that day to encourage her. She writes:

Psalms 139:16
"You saw me before I was born,
Every day of my life was recorded in Your book,
Every moment was laid out before a single day had passed"

Kay, this means to me that there was not one thing we could have done to change what happened. Your time had come. We find comfort in that we could not have protected you from this appointment with death and we were just glad you were prepared for it.

Of course she studied the book of Job and found so many biblical truths that strengthened her faith including how it was the Devil who took Job's children, his health and his wealth. God allowed it to happen but His will for Job was for good and not for harm, but Job couldn't see that it was the enemy who caused all the pain, yet he trusted God. Like Pastor Darrin always taught us, when you can't understand God's hand, you can still trust His heart.

Job just kept getting bad news. He was one of the richest men in the entire region. In one day, he lost 7000 sheep, 3000 camels, 500 teams of oxen, and 500 female donkeys and all ten of his children.

Job 2:10—His wife tells him to curse God and die. But Job replied, you talk like a foolish woman. Should we accept only good things from the hand of God and never anything bad? This was the true test of faith. Can you serve God in the bad times?

Job 3:25—What I always feared has happened to me. What I dread has come true Is there anything worse than losing your children?

Job 42:10—When Job prayed for his friends, the Lord restored his fortunes. The Lord gave him twice as much as before.

In fact if we read on, we see that God does in fact give Job twice as much and he had 14000 sheep, 6000 camels and 1000 oxen and 1000 donkeys. Twice as much. But did you catch the part about the children. He gave Job 10 more children. That was not twice. He already had ten. God doubled everything else but the children. Why? Because Job's children were still alive. They were waiting in heaven. He did have a total of 20.

Mom learned that grief was a journey. It was not linear. You can't say oh, one year or ten years have passed so I am okay now. Grief doesn't have a time clock. It is a minefield and one day you are doing well then something triggers a memory and you are right back in the moment when you first got the news.

We have become accustomed to schedules. Grief doesn't have one. We are told it takes six weeks to recover from surgery or it takes two hours to drive to the city, but grief has its own schedule. The theory that it takes one year to grieve the death of a loved one may have come from the fact that the first year was especially difficult. Grief doesn't have any rhyme or rhythm it simply happens.

Tears are natural, but more difficult for men because of the social stigma that "big boys don't cry." I love it that my dad was man enough to show his emotions and cry without shame. It is important to create a safe environment for men to cry. I sure don't think my dad or brothers are any less alpha male because they cry. Crying was essential to our healing. Tears cleansed the heart. My parents found themselves crying over everything. When they least expected it, tears filled their eyes and made trails down their cheeks.

People should never apologize for crying. Why are we so uncomfortable when someone cries? My mom used to try to hold back tears because she knew it was going to make others uncomfortable and they were going to feel bad because they couldn't console her. Magic words of comfort do not exist. People in grief just want to be understood. So, if you say something simple like, I'm sorry, that means you understand that they are hurting or if you just hug and say nothing, it is okay. They just need you to listen and know that they are understood.

Sometimes the grief would be so intense that Mom would become forgetful and unable to make even simple decisions. She would get lost driving home. She would often forget the ends of sentences or would be unable to remember words or names. She stopped caring how she looked. When the pain was really intense she would get in the back of her dark closet and curl up in a fetal position. Freud would say she was trying to re-enter her mother's womb to the place of protection from hurt and pain. Many nights she couldn't sleep she would drive to my grave in the dark and lie down on the bench beside my grave and cry for me. My mom mourned openly and without shame. She never denied the pain. She may have had tears in her eyes but she would never lose the hope in her heart.

My dad processed his grief by working on something. He had to be doing something. He used his grief energy on a remodeling project or rebuilding one of his old cars. Mom and Dad would have different things that triggered their grief. Familiar sights, sounds and smells can prompted emotions. For instance, Chance and I doubled dated with Mom and Dad to watch "Million Dollar Baby" the summer before my death. This was the last movie that we watched together. Of course, it was a sad movie. Mom loved it, but she has never been able to watch it again. Music was a huge trigger for most people. The right music brought back really strong emotions. Some of the worship music that we used to listen to together was painful and powerful to my mom. My little brother, Matt, liked to listen to the worship songs that I always played. It flooded back memories, but this was a good thing because it helped release the feelings and the brokenness that can lead to healing.

HEALING

As humans we like to feel good. We are good at avoiding pain. We have pain relievers and pain killers, but there was really no avoiding the pain of loss. Many try drugs and alcohol, but the only way through grief is straight through it. There are no short cuts. If you try to avoid the pain you will stop the healing process.

Pour out your heart to God. There will be times when you just sit in His presence without words. Acknowledge who He is. He is the Good Shepherd; the God of all comfort; our hiding place. Claim His promises. Take comfort in His love.

Immerse yourself in God's word. His word will bring strength, hope, comfort and peace. Ask Him to show you a special promise or word of encouragement every day especially when you are having a bad day. Open your heart to His comfort. Write down special verses that are especially meaningful and put them on your refrigerator.

Take care of yourself. If you are like my mom you are trying to take care of everyone else. But your job right now is to survive, everything else can wait. Do what is only absolutely essential at first. It is so important that you learn how to keep healthy boundaries and say no. There are so many expectations that people will place on you especially at holidays. It is important to protect yourself. Practice saying no politely, just a simple, thank you so much, but I am unable to at this time.

Also, put off major decisions for at least a year. The first year is the hardest, although, it does get better. Healing takes time. Along with healing comes clearer thinking. Put off selling the house or changing jobs or giving away significant items. You must have support. Surround yourself with good, healthy, wise, supportive people. Some may also have walked through the valley of grief with you. There will be times when you don't want to talk and that is okay too. If you don't have a grief support group in your community there are some available online. As awkward and uncomfortable as it may be, it is very important for you to talk about the one who is gone. Get into the habit of remembering and sharing little stories with those around you. Laugh. Cry. Talk.

Keep your sense of humor. You will wonder if you can ever laugh again. At first it seems like a betrayal. We think the more morose our countenance, the greater our grief. We can bury that myth. Scripture has said for centuries what medical research is just now validating "a merry heart doeth good like a medicine." (Proverbs 17:22)

Do some physical activity every day. Exercise releases endorphins, the body's natural tranquilizer and mood enhancer. It boosts your immune system and helps you sleep better.

You have probably heard of the "stages" of grief. The word stage seems to imply that a person goes through steps and eventually graduates. The grieving process is more like a series of cycles and is never totally complete. The point of categorizing grief into stages is to let you know what you are experiencing is normal and necessary for your survival and healing.

The first stage is shock and denial. This is a subconscious survival technique to get your through the first part. You are numb. The human body and emotions can only process so much at one time. Gradually, as you become better oriented, this natural Novocain will wear off and reality will begin to sink in. My mom asked Pastor Jared once why she couldn't feel any pain and he wisely told her, "God only gives you as much as you are able to handle right now." If you were able to absorb the totality of the loss, your heart would stop so we have the stage of shock and denial to ease us into it.

Emotional reactions—Don't be surprised at any feeling that arises. The range is wide, intense, and unpredictable. There will likely be anger, guilt, pain, relief, loneliness, anguish, bitterness. Process every feeling in a healthy way. Face it. Feel it. Let it out.

Depression—This is an extended time of being at the very bottom. You are exhausted physically and emotionally. The body needs time to regroup and rebuild. Common during this stage are feelings of despair, hopelessness, and yearning for the one you so loved. If you have any self destructive thoughts, feelings or behaviors you should seek professional help from a pastor or counselor.

Finally, there comes a time when you know your loved one is really gone. Acceptance like every other aspect of healing comes a little at a time. Gradually you will withstand the reality more and for longer periods of time. You will feel pain less often and with less intensity. Crying spells will taper. Eventually you will be able to speak of a loved one in a steady voice. His or her passing will take its rightful place.

The goal of grief recovery is not moving on or getting over it. The goal is to rebuild your world and embrace the memories of both life and death. Mom will never cease to grieve the loss of her daughter, but that doesn't mean she is incapable of engaging in a full and joyous life.

C.S. Lewis states in "A Grief Observed" that one will get over grief, but will never be the same again. "To say the patient is getting over it after an operation for appendicitis is one thing; after he's had his leg off is quite another. After that operation either the wounded stump heals or the man dies. If it heals, the fierce, continuous pain will stop. Presently he'll get back his strength and be able to stump about on his wooden leg. He has 'got over it.' But he will probably have recurrent pains in the stump all his life, and perhaps pretty bad ones; and he will always be a one-legged man. There will be hardly any moment when he forgets it." In the beginning, the gaping wound or the stump will be tremendously painful. Stitches of love, support, happy memories and faith in God will pull the wound together to make it hurt less. As the pain subsides, the patient may be given a prosthesis and learn to walk quite efficiently with it. He may even compensate for his loss by going on to experience greater feats than he would have before the amputation. However, he will never forget that he once had two legs. With enough time only the scar will remain. The scar can serve as a reminder of the intense healing that once occurred. Eventually, looking at the scar will bring about a slight feeling of satisfaction and we may be able to say, "Yes, I did survive this horrendous wound and I am still intact."

Romans 8:28 says "all things work together for good for those who love the Lord and who are called according to His purpose." Yes, there are some good things that come from grief including:

A deeper walk with God
Closer family relationships
Awareness of how much you are loved
Greater appreciation for family and friends
A more accurate perception of the important things in life
New found sensitivity to others' loss
Increase desire to reach out to others
Clearer understanding of life, death and eternity
Strong character, you are a survivor of the worst tragedy.

THE LETTERS

It is also helpful to journal feelings. My mom did this through writing me letters. Here are some of the things she wrote throughout the past seven years.

Kay,

How do you say goodbye or write a tribute to your only daughter? I don't know how to say goodbye or to live without you. We survive, but life will never be the same. I miss you with every beat of my heart and you are never far from my thoughts. I am glad that we lived with no regrets and that the love we shared was always known. Our time together was short but it was wonderful. You continue to be such a source of joy in our lives. We remember you often as we laugh and cry about you daily. We were always so proud of how well you lived your life, which leaves no doubt as to where you are now. I can't imagine having a more perfect daughter. I know when I get to heaven; I can convince God that I did something right when He looks at you. But then again, Dad and I always knew that you made us look good, all we had to do was show up. You made parenting so easy as it seemed you were born good and the rest of us have to work at it. You saw the best in everyone and inspired so many. We have been so blessed by the people in your life who have now become a big part of our lives

and brought us much comfort. You have left such an example and challenge to those you left behind to live as well as you did. As I told you in our last conversation on earth, "I will see you soon."
Love, Mom

Kay,

It's still hard for me to imagine you being in heaven. It seems like you are still off to college and will be home soon. That's the lie I tell my heart so that it doesn't stop beating. But there are times and they are more frequent now that the emotional reality breaks through to my heart and I pray to die to be with you. But then I don't want to disappoint you so I stay strong. God allows us to be so numb by shock at first because our mind could not bear the weight of the truth if our hearts knew that you are gone. Grief, to me, was like waves in the ocean and sometimes there was calm between waves, but then a hard wave will come and it will nearly consume me. You know how I survive it would no surprise to you that it was by faith and grace of God. I have also had a lot of support from friends, yours and mine. I wonder often what you are doing in heaven. There was just so much we still don't know about heaven. I know that there are streets of gold, mansions and the river of life. I think of you exploring all these things with your Papa Jack, who must have been there as you arrived to be your tour guide. I know he was happy to have his baby girl there with him. And, surely you have met Papa Harley and other relatives. I am sure you have made friends with girls from the Columbine shooting that you always admired and that you are Rachel are best friends. And of course, you are still meeting all the heroes of faith in the Bible. I wonder how involved you are in our lives, how much do you see. I know that the book of Hebrews tells us that we are "surrounded by a great cloud of witnesses." I know that you must be in the crowd. And although I don't know that much about heaven I know that Jesus was there and if so then it must be a wonderful place and that you are happy. And that I will spend eternity with you.

One year after my death, my mom celebrated the birthday we shared without me for the first time in 22 years. My birthday was August 16 and hers was August 17. We always celebrated together. She wrote to me:

Happy Birthday Baby! We are making our best effort to continue to celebrate your birthday trusting that you will be here in spirit. This was the first birthday that I have had without you in 22 years but we will smile through the tears and remember you. I have decided to not spend the day in self-pity but to focus on the things for which I am thankful. Here are some of the things that I am thanking God for on your birthday:

1) What a gift you gave your parents by living your life so devoted to God that we never have to even question where you are. It brings us such peace in knowing without a doubt that you are with God and we have the hope of eternity with you.

2) We are thankful for all the relationships that we have gained since your death. It was amazing how God placed people like Coach Pond and Irv in our lives to strengthen us and share our pain. Of course, we are equally thankful for the relationships that were already in place and all the support and love we have received.

3) I am glad that your exit from this world was instantly and without pain. I couldn't bear to think that you may have suffered and I couldn't have been there to comfort you. I know that God was right there with you as you slept in the vehicle and woke up in heaven.

4) *I am grateful that you had such a wonderful life. I thank God that you got to experience every dream. You were such a popular girl, beautiful, smart, the basketball star, and homecoming queen. You were so down to earth and humble about your popularity and understood that God gave you those gifts to draw others to Him.*

5) *I am so glad that there was no unfinished business with us. Our family was always so full of love and happiness. We know that you knew how much love we all shared and there are no regrets and nothing left unsaid.*

6) *I am glad for strength God gave our family to endure such heartache and not be weakened by the situation but become more committed to each other. I think we would make you proud to know that our family has not only survived but by God's grace we have grown closer and stronger through it.*

7) *And most of all I am thankful for every moment with you. It was never enough but of course even eternity will not be long enough with you.*

Happy 22nd Birthday, we will never forget nor stop celebrating your birthday.

Another time later that month Mom had a really weak moment and wrote this letter to me:

Kay, I am trying to be strong. I don't want to disappoint you but right now I would just wish that I could be in heaven with you. I just can't believe that life went on without you but really it hasn't. We only try to stay busy to survive and not think about it. But it doesn't work; tears are always below the surface even when we laugh. What I really miss right now was my prayer warrior. We always encouraged one another. I can just hear you saying right now, "Mom, God will take care of it, He was faithful." Kay, who would have ever thought you would not comb gray hair and give us grandkids with big brown eyes? You always said God orders our steps and we believe that He numbered your days. I can honestly say that I have never questioned God but always knew that one day it would all make perfect sense and we would understand. But if He ordered your steps then He also orders ours and all this must be by His design and I do question God about how did He think I could survive without you I know that you would understand my sadness but know you would say "Mom, you got to be strong for Dad and Matt." So, I promise to pray until my strength is renewed and will keep hoping that you will visit me in a dream. Mom

My future sister in law, Monise Huskey Watson writes on my 22nd birthday:

You're 22 today! Wish you were here to celebrate with us. We miss you sooo much! We are all going to the cabin to celebrate your birthday. We're eating cake too! It's not the same without you here stuffing your face with chocolate and smearing it all over your teeth! Matt and I are going to your grave later to arrange the flowers. I know how much you don't like flowers, but I wanted to honor U and what U meant to us. You have inspired my walk and personal relationship with the God, I have learned so much from you! Thanks for the faith you had and the good you saw in everyone. We will never forget U Love U always

The one-year-anniversary of my death, three weeks after my birthday, Mom writes:

We survived one year when I wasn't sure that I could face the next 24 hours. That awful day will forever be etched in my mind but I also recall the time we had together and the things you said in the days before your death that bring me comfort. I am so grateful that God allowed us to have such a sweet time together the week before your death when I came to college to stay with you. I also remember your last words to me the day of your death when you said you "were going home early" and you thought if you left now you "wouldn't be homesick anymore." I think that was exactly what you did, you have gone home early. I have read lots of books on grief since that day but the one who most expressively describes my emotions was C.S. Lewis. He described grief as being like fear. "I am not afraid, but the sensation was like being afraid. The same fluttering in the stomach, the same restlessness and anxiety." He also described the fog as feeling "mildly drunk." I also share his fear of being alone and dread the moments when the house was empty and I am alone with my grief. I never thought I could live without my children for that was the role I enjoyed the most in life and you made so sweet and easy. I think that God just allowed us all to entertain an angel unaware for 21 years. I could write for days on how your life and death influenced me but suffice it to say that I am changed. Trivial things no longer matter to me; I am more compassionate but also a lot more fragile than before. I hold all things very loosely and eternity was set in my heart more than ever. Now, the official year of mourning has ended and although my heart will never heal, I am asking God to give us joy in this coming year. I know that He promises "beauty for ashes, the oil of gladness instead of mourning, and a garment of praise instead of a spirit of despair." Isa. 61:3 I love you baby. Mom

Mom has learned that each day is a gift and writes about what she would do if she had one more with me:

I was thinking what I would do if I had one more day with you. I wouldn't ask for anything but just an ordinary day of just being with you. I can imagine holding and hugging you as we talked. First, I would want to know all about heaven. Have you seen Jesus, how was your papa and who else have you met in heaven? I would want to know what you do with all your time and how great was the worship there. I would want you to describe how beautiful it was there. So much that I want to know. After assuring myself that you are happy and doing okay I would tell you how we missed you and how hard life was without you. I would tell you how many others have helped us through such a difficult situation. I would tell you how much others loved you and how you could have never imagined how you influenced so many lives. Of course, even though you know it I would tell you countless times how much I love you and how proud I am of you. I would tell you how death was not the end of you and how we keep you alive by talking about you. I would tell you how my heart died with you and how I struggle to continue to find hope of happiness without you. I would tell you how hard it was even now to grasp that you are gone because my heart just can't handle it. Kay, it's the ordinary things that I miss most of all. The days like we had at college before your death when we had so much fun just being together as Mom and little girl. I miss the simple things like you saying "Mom." They're always such sweetness in the sound sort of an excitement to talk to me. One more day but then I would just be asking for just one more. I am liking the thought of eternity . . . just endless one more days with you.

My little brother, Matt was getting married. Mom writes:

Matt proposed last night to Monise. She said YES!!! While it was such a happy occasion I still cried because you couldn't share it with us. The loss of you colors everything we do. Life will just never be same. I was thinking of all the things that died with you. You, who looked so forward to getting married will never, experience that joy. I miss my baby girl. Mom

My future sister in law and friend wrote me this about the engagement:

Hey kAyLa! You would be so excited to know that Matt and I have been officially engaged since October 26!!!!! You would have been so proud of him that night! He was so sweet about the way he asked me! He had a puzzle made with my name on it asking me to marry him:) Of course I said, "Yes!" Now I know why you loved him so much, it's why I do too! It makes me sad to know you won't be here to help us with the wedding plans; you would have had so much fun! Although you'll be in our hearts and in our thoughts I wish you could be here on our wedding day, it won't be the same without you. You loved to laugh and most of all loved to love. Wish life could be as simple and fun as it was for you. You gave life to everyone you knew and everyone you met. I'm glad to have a sister like you! Luv U Kay!!! lOvE, mO

Matt wrote me this note:

Sis, I miss everything about you. I miss having a big sister to take care of me. I wish that I would have gone to all of your games and spent more time with you at college. I am very grateful of all the

wonderful childhood memories we shared together. I have never met another person as pure and holy as you were and I am trying really hard to follow in your footsteps. Not having you here was by far the worst pain I have ever experienced in my lifetime. You will always be a part of my life because I will never forget you.
LOVE YOUR BUBBY

The second Christmas without me, Mom writes me:

Just when you think can't get any worse it does. I came back to work after celebrating my second birthday and anniversary of your death to find out I'm being fired after 13 years of hard work and no previous disciplinarian action despite the constant scrutiny looking for something. See, I'm fearless and that didn't work well with an agency that was run by intimidation tactics and bullying. So after poorly investigating allegation that I broke confidentiality they kick me to curb and treat me like a criminal. Then it gets worse. James Watson decides to test us yet again and this time does the unthinkable. Matt was about to get married and God about to prove His faithfulness.

We always wanted James to stay close to his biological siblings. We had just let him go to Muskogee to see them. Professionally I know that kids act out after visits because they are experiencing grief and loss again but that knowledge goes out the window when it's personal. He came home and began arguing with me. Dad overhears and comes in to tell him "don't disrespect your mother." Now James had always respected pop who he loves dearly. He mainly had issues with me. He has been in fights at school and on the basketball court, but never has he been aggressive in our home. No way . . . We don't even yell at each other . . . This was a sacred, safe place in our home . . . but as Ronnie tells him not to yell at me (Matt was not home at the time thank God or would been brawl) James physically attacks Dad knocks him into the bench and there was blood coming from his ear. Now James had put us through a lot but we stayed committed through all tests. We never cried uncle . . . but this looks like the end. Who could blame us right? We take James to Durant shelter. Dad tells him you have challenged me as a man and there is only going to be one man in this house.

So, I have lost my job, and I am losing another kid because I can't even ask Ronnie to let James come home. Dad was defending me when it happened but oh my heart is breaking. I love James Watson and now I am losing another child. We had no contact with him for a week and even though I won't ask, the one thing Dad can't stand is for my heart to hurt. I just pray. One day Dad says go get my boy and let's go talk to pastor Darrin Begley. James so happy to be home, agrees to work weekly with pastor Darrin and we get a breakthrough we had fought for two years. This was the turning point of the adoption. It was truly a wonderful moment when James who was so vulnerable and scared says pop will you forgive me I give you my word I will never disrespect you again and five years later he had kept his promise.

As for losing my job, I told you God was about to show His faithfulness. I didn't get out of the parking lot from DHS when I got a call from Mays Hospice offering me a job. I challenged my dismissal, through merit protection, won my job back, six months back pay, and record cleared, while I was getting paid by Hospice. I would go on to file a wrongful termination in civil court and win a large settlement (still in appeal court) . . . my son got married, I gained an amazing daughter in law, Monise Watson, made a major breakthrough with James, and got my job back with a nice bonus. We had survived and God brought good out of what the enemy meant for bad. He is so good.

More about the second Christmas without me:

We put up the Christmas tree last night. Of course, we didn't have one last year it was just too hard. But because I want James to have some happy memories of Christmas and he wanted a tree we put it up. It was sad to see all the ornaments you had as a child and we thought you would someday share with your children. We have so many Christmas memories but cry because there will be no more. Anyway, as I was going through that stuff I found the last journal you had written in. I am so thankful that you loved to write. I have things you wrote in seventh grade but I found the last thing you wrote which now seems to be almost prophetic. You were reading "The Purpose Driven Life" again and making notes from it. The last day you had written, "Life on earth was a temporary assignment. Your identity was in heaven and your homeland was heaven." You are finally home, babe, you always knew you didn't belong here. I can't wait till we are all home together.

We made it through another Christmas without you. It doesn't matter how much time passes your death was still as fresh as the day it happened. I still lose my breath, feel faint and panic if I think about it. Matt and I took flowers to your grave for Christmas I was thinking how I would give everything I own just for another moment with you and God just reminded me that I will have all of eternity with you where we will never know pain and separation again. Me, Dad, and the boys went to the cabin and just had a really good time away from everything. My favorite thing was when we ate Christmas dinner, James blessed the food and said "thank you for the family you blessed me with and for all the good memories we have of Kayla." That made Christmas for me. I know that made you smile and that you are so pleased that no matter what we are committed to him and believe that

God's purpose will be fulfilled in his life. Even if I wanted to give up I could never look you in the eye when I get to heaven because of the disappointment that I know would be there. To be honest, I don't know what I would do without him. I told him that when we first adopted him I thought it was God putting him with us because he needed a family but easy to see now that God knew we would need him. I can't wait to hear about your holiday in heaven. Love, Mom

Mom, Dad, and brothers attend senior night at SWOSU. Mom writes:

We went to senior night at SWOSU for what would have been your last college basketball game there. We never dreamed it would end long before this. It was a very emotional time. I don't really know why except that basketball was such a huge part of your life. I am glad we went. Your brothers even made the long trip!! It was great to see all the friends and people who love and remember you. Your impact was still so evident. I notice everyone has that same report about you: how down to earth you were, how you loved everyone and how you were always full of fun. Even though we had a college 15 minutes away offering same scholarship I am so glad that you went to SWOSU. I can't imagine any other place treating your family with so much love and concern even a year and a half later. Of course, Coach Pond was a big reason for this. It was no wonder you loved her so much. I know you would be happy that her family and yours are now very close friends. We share our love for you and the grief of your loss. I am focusing on the fact that the Bible says to "die was to gain" and "to depart was far better" which means you are experiencing far more joy than this world could ever offer.

James and his team win State championship in basketball. Mom
writes:

*Your baby brother just won the state championship. He still wears
the patch with your number 14 on his jersey and says that was why
he plays well. It seems that no matter what joy this world can bring
it we will never truly be happy again without you. I will always
look at everything with the thought of how I wish you were here
to share this moment. You would have been having a ball cheering
for him. I have to believe that God allowed you to cheer him on
tonight from a very good heavenly view but I am sure this was
nothing compared to the joy you are experiencing now with your
King. I miss you baby and hope to see you soon.*

Mother's day 2007. Holidays are such land mines:

*Oh Kay, the pain is still there. Maybe not as forceful as it once
was but it was still there. If I ever stop to allow my heart to absorb
it or something triggers it the pain will come again as intense as
ever. I miss you always. I look at all the cards you gave me for
mother's day in the past and you always wrote to the BEST Mom
in the world. Those were always your words on all your cards.
They sure bring me comfort now knowing that you knew how
much I adored my children. I miss having a daughter. You left
me alone in a house full of men. I love them to death but they will
never share the mother/daughter bond that we had. You know
boys are different. They don't call me ten times a day with every
detail of their life and I miss that. Maybe someday when I am a
grandmother I can recapture that I hope so but still I know it will
never be the same as with you.*

Mom

Mom trying to watch movies of me . . . she still can't do that. It
is too painful:

*Dad and I watched movies of you and Matt when you were small
the other night. It was still so hard to do that. We talked later
that it brings such depressing emotions that we still don't feel like
we are at a point that we can do it. You seemed so alive. It makes
you want to reach out and hug you and remind you how much we
adored you. But even in the midst of the anguish, we are choosing
to allow God to take this unspeakable experience and use it to help
us start to live again. Even though we will forever grieve your loss
I know that you would not want us to lead grief-stricken lives.
We continue to fight to find a place of hope and to focus on the
children we have left behind. I know that was what you would
want for us, but we miss our little girl so bad and it was so hard
to move past the grief.*

Griefshare, the organ donation agency asked my mom to write a
tribute for a story they would feature about me. She titled it, "I
remember . . ."

Kay,

*I remember a tiny infant fighting for her life weighing only 2.5
pounds at birth.*

*I remember I couldn't hold you because you because you were
hooked up to tubes and I would sit for hours just rubbing your
little hands and feet.*

*I remember the sweetest little brown eye girl who wanted to
tell her Mom endlessly how much she loved her. I even remember
saying, Kay, let's don't tell Mom so much.*

I remember you walking to class at Kindergarten with your pooh bear holding an "I love you sign" behind your back all the way to the room to show me you loved me.

I remember a shy, insecure little girl who felt that she didn't have any friends and was afraid of missing a day of school because her one friend, Mindy might quit talking to her. Oh, I remember all the pain of growing up.

I remember you changing schools to Stringtown and going from having no friends to one of the most popular kids in school.

I remember you moving to Tushka as a freshman and being intimidated by all the senior athletes.

I remember you being so strong in your convictions that even as a freshman you stood strong in your Godly values even though it wasn't the popular thing to do.

I remember praying on your way to school that Coach Hall wouldn't say too many negative things to you.

I remember your first heartbreak when Sean Hall broke up with you. I remember us just driving around and talking, just to try to pass the time until your heart could heal. I remember leaving work abruptly just because my little girl was home crying and I would come home and we would drive somewhere.

I remember you met Matt Phillips and how much a part of our family he became. I remember your struggle when you broke up with him after like 3 years. I remember your vow not to date for one year to give him time to heal.

I remember you becoming a basketball star and how determined you were to make sure to use your talent to glorify God.

I remember you wouldn't go to graduation or prom parties because there would be drinking there. I remember you coming home after prom to eat grilled cheeses at Aunt Treba's with Jen.

I remember your compassion for people. I remember how accepting and excited you were that we were adopting James.

I remember your love for Matt and how angry would you get if you ever felt that anyone was mistreating him.

I remember how you and I used to love to aggravate Dad and all the laughter we shared in our home.

I remember the day you left for college and I prayed God would give me grace. I remember that you were so happy with college and that we became even closer after you moved away.

I remember that you insisted that I learn to text message so we could stay in contact while you were in school.

I remember you coming home on weekends and I would pamper you. I remember how you loved to just be with the "fam" and how you loved to double date with me and Dad.

I remember what a sweet time we had the week before your death when I came to stay with you at college.

I remember that you wanted me to take you to class and then come and get you. You said, "Mom, it's just like I'm your little girl again."

I remember how the shy insecure little girl grew into a woman full of grace and beauty with so much confidence in herself and her purpose in life.

I remember your compassion for elderly and underprivileged children.

I remember how you believed the best about people and brought out the best in them. I remember you being in love with Chance and not willing to give up on him.

I remember that the day before your death you telling me "I am so ready to go to heaven."

I remember you saying goodbye that day and making me promise that I come see you soon.

I remember hearing from a friend the awful news that you had been in an accident and refusing to believe that you would be seriously hurt.

I remember driving so fast to try to get there and yet if felt like it was taking forever.

I remember being told that my baby girl was dead and how my heart immediately died also.

I remember thinking how will I ever live one day without my precious baby girl.

I remember how I tried to take care of everyone else and fulfill your wishes regarding arrangements.

I remember waking the next morning to the worst day of my life and your Dad asking me, "Will we make it through this they say losing a child causes so many to divorce?" I remember saying, yes, we will make it who else could ever understand the depth of this experience. No one but me and you.

I remember a wonderful memorial service both at SWOSU and Atoka. I can't recall too many funerals where you left uplifted but yours was like that because of a life so well lived.

I remember getting to know people who you were close to and how much they helped by sharing our grief.

They say a mother's heart is the best camera. I remember everything about you.

My little sister, Charisma Chloe who became a part of our family in 2007, two years after my death, Mom wrote:

Kay, you have a little sister and I have a daughter. God always surprises us. I always wondered what would happen after this year. James is going to college at Washington State and Matt is getting married in December. It is going to difficult for someone who has to nurture but I have been through tough times and confident I would adjust. Anyway, out of the clear blue, God blesses us with another child. It has to be God for Dad to agree and he is smitten with her. Dad says this is the happiest I have been since you have been gone. I am glad that I get another chance to be Mom. It is definitely a different lifestyle for me, but I am enjoying her so much. We tell her about her sister. We show her pictures and she has taken flowers to your grave. You would love her. She reminds me so much of you. She has such a gentle heart and spirit and extremely affectionate. She is just what I needed. God is so good. She is a beautiful 3 year old black girl. She will help us heal. I think I am a better, more patient Mom this time around. Either way I have someone else to help fill the emptiness in my heart. It still hurts and I have missed having a daughter so much. Dad reminded me that you wrote shortly before your death how you wanted to adopt a little black girl so I'm happy we are fulfilling your dream.

Christmas 2008, Mom writes:

I still can hardly do this. It makes me so sad that you are not home for holidays. Nothing will ever change the fact that we miss you terribly. No matter how we try to fill the void you simply are constantly on my mind. Charisma (Rizzy) knows so much about her sister because we talk about you endlessly. She is so enamored with Christmas. We went shopping and as we came out of the bathroom she sees an angel with other decorations as she says, "oh, mommanet (that's what she calls me) it's Kayla's angel . . . Kayla would like that for her grave, can we buy it for Kayla's grave and so you will have a $24 angel on your grave for Christmas because Rizzy wanted it for her sister. It is so sweet. The other night she was lying on the bed and was just staring at the stars you put on the ceiling. After about ten minutes I said, "What are you thinking about Rizzy," and she said, "Kayla, I'm just missing Kayla." She has already shared our heart for you. We always talk about how much you would love her and how good you would be with her.

You will meet her someday as I can already tell she has such a heart for God. Hopefully, we will nurture that and she will walk in the spiritual steps of her big sister.

Mom rarely dreams of me, but I visited her once and she writes:

I dreamed of you last night. I rarely get that privilege and am always thankful when God allows you to visit in my dreams. You were playing basketball and I was talking about how hard it was to watch you because you seemed so alive (this was during the dream) but after the game I went to talk to you even though I knew it would be hard to say goodbye again and I knew you were dead, but I hugged you and it was so real. I woke up before we had to say goodbye. I was crying and Rizzy asks why so I was telling her about the dream. She is so perceptive spiritually (just like you were) she says "Kayla was praying for me, she prayed Jesus let me live with you." Wow, out of the mouth of babes . . . You remember how you would say Mom, guess what and I would say what and you would say I love you, and you would wear me out doing it over and over. Well, now Rizzy has her own version of that circular conversation. She asks me endlessly who you love? She then wants me to say everyone but her so she can say you forgot me . . . and laugh. Then ask me again and again. I miss you. You should be here for the wedding. Even the happiest times have sorrow because you can't share it.

Matt's wedding:

Kay,

I know you had a huge smile in heaven when your adored little brother married Monise last weekend. There was suppose to be a picture of you on the stage and there was a slide show of you and Matt with a song he picked out "once in a while" by Billy Dean. Neither of them worked out for the wedding or reception and I felt like that was probably best and you wouldn't have wanted any sadness for Matt on that day. Nice try, but we all thought of you. When Pastor Darrin gave the blessing on them he talked about how proud you would be of him and Matt struggled not to cry. Most of the rest of us gave in to tears at that point. Matt told me later how hard that was for him not to cry. Like Pastor Darrin said Matt has shown such godly character in the face of adversity and stayed true to his faith and chose to walk in love and forgiveness when we lost you. Dad and I just feel so blessed by all of our children. It was a beautiful wedding and they are so happy. Would have been a perfect day had we not missed you . . .

THE ACHE IS STILL THERE

My mom read this poem recently in Compassionate Friend's Newsletter and felt that it so poignantly described how they feel about me.

The Ache We Hold Inside

When these children we loved are taken and the years pass slowly by,
You feel the grieving was over But the ache was still inside.
This life of ours must continue and the tears we must learn to hide
But you know it will never leave you, This ache we feel inside.
Their siblings go on with their futures and you know this was how it should be.
You share in their joys and sorrows, but that ache won't let you free.
Where they rest, you visit less often and their voices are not so clear,
and our zest for life was returning, but the ache was always near.
Our friends and family tell us how well we handled our grief If they only knew deep within us from this ache there was no relief.
When alone we talk to them often, for we know they are still by our side and the warmth of our memories comfort but the ache will always abide.
As we continue this earthly voyage and the calm and storms pass by we will cherish our precious memories and this ache we hold inside.

You are greatly loved and missed.
Love, Mom and everyone's heart you touched.

Mothers Day 2008, Mom wrote:

Mother's day, Memorial Day, James' graduation. All without you and never easy because of that. The boys were sweet and did their best but no one could ever make me feel as loved and valued as a Mom as you did. Don't think for one moment that I have moved on and forgot about you. You are omnipresent in my mind. I miss you every moment of every day. I know if you could speak to me you would say finish the work God called you to do and I will but He knows that the moment I am done I'm headed home. O happy day.

James leaving for college at Washington State in June of 2008:

It's done Kay. He left for WSU this morning. Me, Dad, Matt, Mo, Rizzy, and James spent the weekend in Dallas prior to his leaving today. We had a magical family time but I cried every time your name was mentioned and other times when I just thought of you because you should have been with us. Our family was just not the same without you. You would be so proud of James. He has matured so much. He loves having a family. You would have been smiling as Dad cried when James hugged him bye. You would have laughed at Matt giving big brother advice. Rizzy refused to hug or say goodbye because she "doesn't like James' getting mommanet's lovins." She was ready for him to get to college. He was so excited, reminds me of you when you left. My sadness at his departure was only equaled by my excitement for him and relief that he made it!! We had a lot of bumps along the way but we never gave up. I sat at your grave in the middle of the night so many times begging God to release me from him because it was just too painful to love him. He never would and I couldn't disappoint Him or you (of course, the fact that I love

131

James immensely didn't hurt either). Its' hard to fail when you have the King of the Universe holding your hand, but there were times when all I hung to was the fact that I made a commitment to God to love this boy and give him a family. Now, we get to see the fruit of that commitment. He was wearing your number in college to honor you. How sweet was that? And He has grown so much spiritually. I had believed God for total surrender to Him before he left our home and He did not disappoint. James was there. That alone makes this story have a happy ending. I know I have heard people say that I just use James and Rizzy to fill the void you left. Maybe so? Is that a bad thing? Some lose children and turn away from God, choosing to fill void with anything that will relieve the pain (drugs, alcohol) but I chose to fulfill God's call on my life to nurture. You know I love being a Mom. I think you would be pleased with how I tried to cope with the unbearable loss of my beloved daughter.

My 24th birthday in August of 2008:

Kay,

We will never stop celebrating our birthdays although it was not as happy as they once were. We joined the Ponds in the city and watched movies of you, ate cheesecake and remembered the sweetest little girl a Mom could ever hope for. Dad and I spent a long while at your grave last night, remembering and thanking God that we had Cinderella for 21 years. We survive because we know you are happy. God gave me a thought yesterday during my tears that if I recall some of the best times I have had in God's presence one thing I know was that I never want to leave that moment because it was such a happy, peaceful feeling and if I take that feeling and multiply it by a million then maybe I'm getting close to how happy you are in the very presence of our King. We know that God still has a purpose for us here and we will fulfill that call but we long for the day when we will all be together again and once again our family will know true happiness.

The third anniversary of my death, Mom writes:

In some ways it does seem quick but most of the time it feels like I have lived a lifetime without you. I remember thinking how will I live one day without her and here we have survived three years. I wonder if I am better or worse than at first. I feel like Job who said that "the thing I feared worse has now come upon me." My child was gone. The pain still there, and there are times when something will trigger my grief and I descend into this deep depression that was so hard to press through. I finally made the decision to start seeing Pastor Jared and to get some help because I can't live like this any longer. It's time to let God heal the wound. That's what you would want. For your anniversary I read "The Shack." A story much like ours and it helped. God still has an abundance of grace and he just flooded my mind on this day of happy memories that I had not thought of it in a while. like when you surprised me coming home after telling me you couldn't come because of practice. I remember crying when you came in the door. I remember you driving all night to attend Matt and James' game. You were just the complete package, such a Godly girl, so thoughtful, but yet so full of fun and laughter. I pray that joy can return to my life and I can learn to live again. I know I can't get over it but hopefully I can learn to live with it. I know God has grace for that too. I miss you more with every passing day. Mom

The third Christmas without me:

Christmas means family get together huh and that magnifies our loss. Three Christmases and I guess God has healed the wound and we are doing good on this journey of grief but then holidays come and tears just seem to always spill over. We are going to Baton Rouge where James and the team will be so the whole family will be together except for you. I wish I could see you just for a moment. Dad and I were out eating last night and both just sitting there not saying anything and both just start crying. That's been the good thing about our shared loss we always understand each other's thoughts and moods. We miss you terribly. We will be making our trip by your grave before we leave town. We will always remember you.

My 25th Birthday:

Kay,

We celebrated your birthday by watching videos of you and took flowers to your grave and just spend time remembering the sweetest little girl ever. We later went to watch scary movie for you and had dinner at your favorite, Johnny Carinos. Tonight on my birthday we have chocolate cake decorated for you and saying we thank God every time we remember you. We are going to eat chocolate cake and get it all in our teeth just like you used to love to do for laughs. We miss you terribly. It seems there was just always a void that can't be filled without you. You know Matt's baby will be here soon and he was determined to honor you by naming her after you. So many kids are named after you . . . Cassie's little girl was Rayleigh Kay. Jen has Harley Beth. Matt and Mo will name our little girl Kayden Elizabeth . . . This alone reminds me that your life matters and your influence will continue. I am also reminded every Sunday at church when I see at least all your friends who moved here to attend your church. It was all connected to you and you continue to inspire others with your passion for God. As for your Mom I try to honor your life by loving and helping others but I still long for the day when I will once again be united with the one who loved me so perfectly. On that day we will be as though we were never apart and I didn't have to suffer one day without my baby girl. I will not waver in my faith in God but wonder if I will ever recover emotionally from the loss of you. I love my little girl . . .

Four years after my death, Mom writes:

Kay,

How silly of me to think people would forget you. The one common theme about your life was you loved . . . you loved God you loved family you loved coach pond and all your friends throughout your life you even loved people who did you wrong you loved everyone . . . that flowed from your relationship with God . . . and that love was eternal . . . it remains long after you have gone. I know that I can say that love we experience was so pure and it's a rare experience to share that with anyone in this life. I was also thinking about home and how much you always loved your home . . . always enjoyed coming home the place of love joy and comfort . . . and now you are truly home . . . the place prepared just for you . . . this was all temporal and someday we are coming home. No regrets Kay . . . we will love people and life just like you . . . love mommy

Matt's baby, my niece, Kayden Elizabeth was born and Mom writes:

Kayla,

By now you are an aunt of three days. Kayden Elizabeth your niece was born Oct 15. It's taken me awhile to post this because of the emotion attached to it and difficulty to really articulate what I want to say. She was precious and we are so happy to have her. But as with everything else it makes me wish you were here to share this experience. Matt was determined that she would be named after you. So many others are named after you. Jennifer has Harley Beth. Cassie has Ryleigh Kay. Brad Huffman's daughter named Kayla and now Kayden Elizabeth. I pray that each one share your heart for God and passion for His kingdom. Your memory lives on and you continue to inspire another generation with your life. I love you Kay. I still miss you so much. I hold Kayden and can't help the tears as I remembering holding the sweetest little girl in the world. If only I had known how soon it would all end . . .

Merry Christmas 2010:

Kay,

We are about to take your flowers to the grave. Don't ever think for one moment that we have forgotten you. You are with us always and constantly in my thoughts. God has been good to us this year and continues to give us strength to live through the grief of missing you. We were so blessed this year to have miraculous healing of James' heart after being told he couldn't play sports. We were also blessed with a sweet grandbaby. James got to come home for Christmas which was a story straight out of "Trains, Planes and Automobiles" and was such a joy to have him home for a few days

(2). He was my gift and Dad had your pearl necklace remade and with some of your diamond earrings in a heart . . . very beautiful and very thoughtful and sweet.

5 years, 2010:

It has been five years . . . this should be getting easy right? It was amazing how I find myself fighting against that dark pit of depression that was calling me just with your birthday and anniversary of death coming up. It all started with keeping your niece, Kayden. Oh my, how she reminds me of you and Matt so much. She spent her first night with us this week. I rocked her and cried and remembered the sweetest baby in the world I once held not so long ago. Then I wanted to show Matt how much she looked like you so I got pictures out and that end result was not pretty eyes swollen, nerves shot and deep depression. I still just have so many emotional issues related to losing you. I find myself putting up walls with Kayden because I just can't bear to get close to her and risk the loss and pain again. I guess even though I feel that God has sustained and grown me in this I will always suffer the wounds of losing my baby. I love you Kayla. I am still fighting

5 years letters from my brothers:

James:

I am missing you so much right now . . . I think about you every day and just wish you were here to see how much I have accomplished and how basketball was going. Oh, and how buff I am now. Back then I was skinny as a stick. You would be proud of me sis . . . There is no one in this world who could take your

place. You were so happy that you had me as a brother and I was super happy to have you as my sister . . .
Love and miss you sis

Matt:

Hey Kay, I sure miss ya. It's been 5 years now but it seems like it was yesterday. Yea time is really flying by. I am a Dad now and she looks just like me and you. You would really enjoy her. I wish you were here so you could have kids of your own and they could play together. Well I hope you are having a good time in heaven. I love you and I will be seeing when it's my time to go.

Random letter from my mom:

Kay,

I'm going through a wave of grief lately. I thought it would help if I expressed my emotions by writing you. I am just missing you. You expect these times at holidays and anniversaries but you just never know what will trigger an episode of just intense grief. I'm just wondering did you know, really know how much I loved you? In the end it all that matters, did you love and were you loved. That and God is all that matters. I have no doubt about your relationship with God and you are still inspiring and influencing people. Nathan is moving down here now. Isn't that awesome! 4 people from your college now being fed at your church . . . because of you . . . but that makes me cry too because you were so amazing spiritually. I just can't fathom today that I am never going to see you again on this earth. That still seems impossible. Don't worry, I don't grieve as those who have no hope and God will grant me peace but still the hole in my heart the size of Texas can't be filled.

I miss my daughter desperately. I wish I could just see you. Just a glimpse, even if I couldn't talk to you or hold you if I could just see you for a moment. We go through things in life at work or whatever and it just never bothers me. I think nothing compares to losing you, all else is a walk in the park compared to living each day without the sweetest daughter ever. I miss you always. Mom

Christmas, 2011:

Why can I not stop crying at Christmas? We skipped Christmas gifts and opted for a trip out of town. We are in San Antonio. Matt, Monise, Kayden, James and Rizzy are with us. Everyone but you and my heart breaks. I just want you. It seems my life would be perfect if only I had you. Nothing material means anything without you. The void has never been filled and my heart will ache until I see you again. But I am thankful for the gift of God and that He was Immanuel (He was with us) if not for that there would be no hope. You were a gift Kay. You were always so sweet and thoughtful to me and really to everyone, but you made us all feel special. I love you forever and miss you with every beat of my heart. Merry Christmas. I am sooo thankful that you are safe at home.

MORE HEALING

In January of 2011, God did something amazing in my family. A few weeks before Pastor Darrin had given my dad a word about how there was going to be healing in our family. My dad really didn't know what he was referring to, but he thanked God and began to get in agreement with this prophesy. Amazingly, against all hope, God restored my dad's relationship with my sister, Kary Jo. I mentioned earlier that I had a sister from my dad's first marriage. It was a bad divorce and Kary grew up without a father's love. I hated that for her. I prayed that those scars would be healed someday soon. I tried to get to know Kary after we were adults, but there was still healing that needed to be done. We shared e-mails and Chance and I would have lunch with her some months before my death. I am so thankful that I got to see her. I always wanted to know my big sister so you can't imagine how happy I was when my parents were able to reconnect with Kary. I like to think that I planted some seeds for the eventual reconciliation. Kary was so sweet and it was as if she had always been a part of us. Mom says she has my tender heart. She is such a thoughtful person. Matt was so excited to have a sister again. Dad squeezed Mom's hand on the way back from their first meeting with Kary and said, "We have one daughter back." Mom had only known the heartache of losing one little girl but he had lost two . . . one to death and one to divorce. God restored Kary and I am safe at home where we will spend all eternity. God is so good.

6 year anniversary September, 2011, Mom writes:

Kay I love you. I miss you. Never a day passes that I don't remember you in a hundred different ways. If only . . . we talked last night what would you think of our lives six years later. I think you would love Rizzy. I think you would be good for her. She has been good for me. She loves me like you. So wants her Mom's love and attention. She was also great at hugs and loving me. So she has helped me cope. I hope that we honor your memory by our lives. I know that we have changed but hopefully in positive ways. Material things hold very little joy now. Family time means much more. But in matters of faith we remain steadfast and unchanged. I never question God just trust His heart and know that someday when I get to hold you again all will make perfect sense. Until that day . . . Mom

Summer 2012, Mom writes:

Matt and I have been going to this six week bible study with at church on Tuesday nights. Pastor Darrin was teaching. Matt was finally picking up your passion for God. I never doubted he would. He has always been a good godly example of living holy but now he has developed such an intimacy in his relationship with God. He calls me to talk about God all the time. He tells me what he read and prayed about in his devotional time. He was listening to Christian music and he wants to witness to friends. Sounds like you huh? We have been sharing so much about you and your walk with God. I am so blessed to have Godly kids like

*you and Matt. I was just extremely blessed. So, so thankful . . .
and Kayden she has a heart for worship just like you. She will
already raise her hands and worship . . . so sweet . . . your legacy
lives on . . . Thanks for being such an inspiration to all of us . . .
love and miss you!*

MEMORIES FROM FRIENDS
AND TEAM AT SWOSU

"The memory of the righteous is blessed . . ." (Philippians 1:3)

C oach Pond gave Mom a book of memories that our team and different friends from college had written:

Kayla's freshman year, my sophomore year, we went Kayla's house almost every weekend because she was so homesick. Kayla wasn't my roommate the first semester. She came because we already had roommates so she came over to my dorm and we both slept in my twin size bed.

Well this one time we sat around and made up jokes that didn't have point to them so we could get people to laugh and then tell them that it didn't have a point. One of our favorite things to do this summer was drink energy drinks and conquer Mario with Mark and Chance. Kayla farted one time at the gym and it was so bad that she stayed on one end of the gym while we all went to the other end. I'd say "she cleared the gym."

Kayla Horn

Watson was an awesome girl and an awesome friend. I probably never would have made it through my freshman year without her.

She could always put a smile on my face no matter what mood I was in. She was my weight lifting partner and she would to sing to me and anyone else to help us get through our workouts. After I left the basketball team, I didn't see her often, but when I did she always smiled and gave me a huge hug. I'll never forget how big a heart she had and how much love she gave to me and everyone else around her. I know I'll miss her, but I also know I'll never forget the great times I had with her. I feel so lucky to have had her in my life. Kristy Kurtz.

I am so glad that I got the chance to know Kayla. Even though I only got to know her for a short time her friendship and love of Christ meant so much. She will always be missed but never forgotten. Love ya! KW

Janet Marks

To the Watty family, I loved Watty very much. She was such a wonderful person. I enjoyed being around her and especially when got to play together. I'll never forget it. I and Watty were probably the best nap takers ever. 3 hour naps are great. I also enjoyed all the pictures she drew of me with my big hair. I'll cherish them forever. Love ya! B #5 (Bethanie Benz)

I'll never forget hearing that sweet voice and I'd turn around and say, "Kayla!!! Whataya doing?!? We'd hug each other and no matter how bad my day was or how tired I was, I would be so happy and so full of energy when I saw her. What I'll remember most about Kayla was how she'd say "I LOVE YOU!" in a sincere, child like way and her brown eyes would just twinkle. I also remember the time at one of our dorm meetings she told me (she made up a story) that she fell asleep in the bathroom (on the toilet) one night for several hours and Kayla had to come and get her. She told me this because I was embarrassed about falling asleep in our dorm lobby all night. I remember her singing with all her heart to Jesus @BASIC on Thursday night. I remember a late night trip to IHOP☺ I remember her carrying her Bible everywhere she went. There have been times that I didn't want to be here at school, but I would think of "kaylas" and I would get excited to come back. This happened so many times, even this year. I love and miss her so much. I'm not scared any more, in fact I'm excited about the day when I will see her in heaven and can say, "Kayla, what are you doing?!? I LOVE YOU! ☺ It's hard for me to imagine, but I believe she'll be even more perfect and more beautiful than she was on earth. I looked up to her so much and I hope my life will glorify Jesus and radiate His pure, precious love as much as Kayla's did. Love Laura Leigh Altom

When we were freshmen I would see Kayla in the training room all the time and she always smiled and said "hey." Even this one time in the cafeteria I was sitting by myself and she said, "Hey, you can come sit with us. Those times were before I knew her or met but I knew there was something about her that made me want to be around her. She was so fun, special, caring and had God radiating from her. The first time we truly hung out/met was on the SWOSU Palouse (our freshman year) my friend I were walking around and ran into Kayla and some of her friends. From there we went (walked) to Braums' and then back to Steward Hall. After hanging out that night my life did a 180 turn. One week later, Kayla and Kayla Horn led me to Christ. I love her so much and I'm so thankful that I ended up here at SWOSU because I got to meet and hang out with such an outstanding role model, leader, and friend. Words can't describe how much I love her and the impact she had on my life. From the day I met Kayla, I knew she was a special girl. She had a way of lifting up people and brightening their lives. I don't know if it was her smile, her perky attitude or a combination of the two. Whatever it was it was amazing. Kayla was not your average person. She had so much spirit and heart and love for others. Those are not traits possessed by many people. I know Kayla is in a better place now; a place of peace and happiness. She served her purpose very well while she was here with us on earth. But her time came and now she is with God whom she loved so very much.

Love Chelsea Edwards.

K was an awesome person, she put her whole heart into everything she did, whether it was studying, playing basketball or woshipOping and severing the God she loved so much. Kayla was an amazing role model and it was not usually the words that she said but more importantly it was the way she lived. She always had a smile on her face and if people around didn't then she would find something funny to do or say just to make them laugh. One thing I will never forget about Kayla was the big smile she would have on her face after she made a shot. Kayla and I never had any deep talks but we would always say hello and anytime she would always say "I love you" and many people could say this and not mean it but I know that she meant it every time. Kayla was an outstanding Christian who lived every moment for Christ. I love and I will never forget her.

Loriane Weekley

Kayla truly was a unique person that I was so blessed to have known for two years. Whether she was just relaxing in the lobby or busting a 3 pointer, she always had a huge smile on her face. She also made a point to tell everyone that she loved them multiple times a day. Actions like these are contagious in a good way. One thing that people know about Kayla was that she didn't care what other people thought about her appearance, actions or um bodily functions. However, she cared a great deal about what other people thought about her Lord. She had an unashamed passion for Jesus that challenged all of us in so many ways. Even in her death, I am encouraged to live like her because she strived to live like Jesus. Your daughter was amazing. Thank you for the blessing.

Larissa Maines

Wow! What can you say about Kayla? Words honestly can't even describe how awesome she was! When we would play silent football, you're not allowed to smile, so needless to say, she was always the first one out 'cuz she couldn't help but to constantly smile. This one time when we played volleyball, she got this spurt of energy that would make her act and look like an excited 5-year-old. She ran in circles in the sand, kicked it up and then fell back on her back kicking like a four year old throwing a temper tantrum and then would get still and then would make a sand angel. She was so childlike—From her pure heart to her personality to her faith and trust in the Lord and people. She always expected the best in everybody. You would always want to be good and Christ like person around her. Not because she would condemn you if you didn't because she wouldn't do that but because she knew your heart and would want you to and you never wanted to disappoint Kay. She was inspiring and caring. I've never in my life met anyone like her. Oh and one more memory. Last year I went to Texas with Kayla Horn, Jessica Bailey and the twins. We went to Texas to say with Baileys and we were going to come back up through and stay at Wattys. I was so tired of health food by the time we got to Kay's, so right when we got there she ate some Oreos with me. It was great. She always wanted people to feel comfortable and happy. I love her so much. I will miss her. She was the greatest.

Tisha Burns

To Family and friends of Kayla
From Nikki Sloan

I would tell you how special your daughter, sister, friend Kayla was but I know you already know. Kayla loved to make people smile and she was good at it. We were I guess the "hicks" of the team. Everyone would make fun of the way we talked, especially when we said the word "drank." Kayla was my van buddy on road trips. She would always put her feet up on me and get a nice long nap (oh how she loved her naps) while I would have to study for class. Kayla, Kayla Horn and I would sometimes sing the song "this little light of mine" on road trips. Kayla W (Watty) would be lead singer and Kayla Horn and I would be the backup singers "Oh, let it shine sister, let me see that light." Let me tell you we had some soul! I don't know what this next basketball season has in store, but it will all be for Kay! She will always have a special suit on our team and a special place in my heart. I am really going to miss her for countless reasons. Kayla had a way of making everyone around her feel important and special. Her smiling face could brighten anyone's day. Everyone in the dorm adored her, because she exuded God's love to everyone. I never once heard Kayla say a bad word about anyone, but I always saw her build people up. She dearly loved and her family and was so proud to adopt her brother. The first day of school this year we had lunch together and talked about our summers and our plans for the future. Basically, Kayla's plan for the future boiled down to loving people and ministering to them for the Glorify of God. Surely Kayla fulfilled that in her life. She has been an example and an encouragement to me in my walk with God. She will never be forgotten.

Kayla was beautiful inside and out. Her inner beauty was what I loved most of all. I miss you,

Kay! Love you Watty,

Niki Sloan SWOSU #31

Kay was an amazing best friend. I have never met anyone like her. Anytime Kay told me she was going to do something, she did it, she always kept her word. I know that when Kayla came here to SWOSU that she was going to be someone very special and close to me. We hit it off great from the very beginning. I enjoyed very much going home with her on weekends. I love your family very much and am so glad I got to know y'all. I know that she helped my relationship with God very much. Kay was one of the people that taught me that "God can't be put in a box, He can do anything he want and I have to be open minded to think things I wasn't' taught in church." I thank Kay for being my best friend and am blessed to have her in my life. She would be so excited when her Mom came to visit. Oh, she was so excited this last time she came to visit Kay because her Mom took off work to come and stay with her for a week. She loved her family very much and talked about them very often. But most of all God was the number one person in her life. I am so blessed to have had such a best friend like that. I love her very much and miss her very much. I love your family and still want to come to visit. Thank you for everything.

In Christ, Kayla Horn

Kayla Watson, it's hard to just say one thing about her. It would take up so much paper to try and explain how she will always mean to me. She was probably the best 3 point shooter I ever saw. When we played basketball it was always a relief to know that she was on my team so she couldn't "light us up." I don't know if I actually ever sit down and think about what people mean to me, but I have thought about Kayla a lot. I've come to realize that I love her so much and I want to be like her. She had the sweetest spirit and the most wonderful smile. She was so giving, too. I remember I didn't have an alarm clock and she said she would wake up early to make sure I was up. I had an 8 o'clock class and her first class wasn't until 9:00. That always meant a lot to me, because I know I wouldn't volunteer to wake u an hour early. I love you, Kayla and I miss you. I hope I can be like you, even if it was just a little bit.

Who am I going to talk about nutrition to? Kayla always wanted to know what was "healthy" and what wasn't, she'd call this summer sometimes just to ask if she could eat a particular food. Kayla was after God's hear; it was obvious. She exhibited all the fruits of the Spirit so genuinely. I will miss her deeply. She was truly an angel!

Love, Grace Anne #10

I have had this book for a while not knowing what to say. Kayla was an amazing person. Because of her, I have changed my outlook on life. I want to be a better person. I want to be like Kayla. This was still really hard for me. I'm trying to say everything that I have been thinking and feeling but Kayla was so great I can't put it all down. She never judged anyone, she liked you for who you were, not what she heard about you, but who she got to know and care about. Kayla lived every day to the fullest. She lived it just like God wanted her to. It's crazy because I only knew Kayla for one year. In that first year, she taught me so much. I just wish I could have told her how much she taught me, how much she touched my life. I was blessed for getting to know her, for the short time I did. Before I finish I would like to share some memories that make me smile every time I think about them. Kayla and I were a few of the lucky ones who got to attend study hall! And let me tell you, I have never in my whole life enjoyed study hall so much! We did study; really, we would just help each other out sometimes. I'll never forget Kayla had a play she had to read and she got me to do the parts with her. And we had to be voices. We made it through a page and a half and realized we were using a male voice for a *female. So, we started all over and did it right ☺ I loved Kayla so much. She was truly an angel on earth. She's home now and happy. She was missed, but never forgotten. I love you Watty!*

Love always, Briana Harris SOSU #23

It's been really hard for me to make myself write in this. There are just so many things to say about Kayla that words cannot explain. She truly was a blessing from God. She was the type of person that just makes you want to be a better person. I remember when she talked to me about a few things and told me that she looked at me as leaded and looked up to me. In a way that made me happy, but also broke my heart because I knew that I should have been the one looking to her and following the same path she did. Kayla had a way of making everyone feel welcome. She had a connection with everyone she met. Everyone she met felt special and she could make anyone feel like her best friend. I can never think of a moment when I was sad around Kayla. She always made me smile no matter what she was doing whether it was eating with her mouth wide open, having that cheesy smile on her face, playing basketball or oh man that pony tail of hers. Every day she came into practice (probably just waking up from a 3 hour nap) I would ask if she had brushed her hair that day. I can still picture that lumpy ponytail that so little with strays hanging out everywhere. Kayla touched many lives in many different ways. You raised a wonderful daughter that loved you very much. She could never stop talking about her family. You all meant the world to her. I will never forget playing with Kayla. I always knew when she shot if she was going to make it or not. She had this look in her eye that she knew if she had the ball she could hit a 3 from 10 feet behind the line. Then she would take off running down the court with the biggest smile you've ever seen. I remember when she would just look at us and say "I'm on fire." That meant to give her to the ball. She would say as if she couldn't help it, all her shots were just going in. I went to their first conditioning practice on the track and I hadn't seen Kayla since she was back for school. As soon as I walked up she came over to me and gave me this huge hug and told me that she loved me. I loved her hugs. She would always squeeze you so tight as if she was never going to let you go. I loved Kayla so much. My life has changed since knowing Kayla. She has touched many lives and made many people happy even if it was recording their farts on her phone. I thank God for bringing her into this world every day. I want to thank her family for everything they have done. There are so many great stories I could share but I'd need 100 more books. I will always love Kayla and miss her so much. She is an angel! I LOVE YOU!

Paige Adams.

Words cannot express how much I admired Kayla Watson. She had such an impact on my life. Her outlook she had on life seemed to be contagious. I always looked forward to her coming around that corner to my office. She could always put a smile on my face no matter what was going on at work or at home. I have never met anyone like her and probably never will. Kayla was such an amazing teammate. I know every person on our roster absolutely loved her. She was such an encourager. There were plenty of times she could have been angry with a teammate but chose not to, you don't find kids like Kayla Watson. I think about her every day at least a 100 times a day. Everything I do seem to remind of her in some way. I am so glad I had the opportunity to get to know her. Because of her I have a closer relationship with God. I talk to Him every day and ask him to tell Kayla hello and that I love and miss her. There are so many stories involving Kayla. I only knew her for two years and have more great memories about her than people I have known a lot longer. Ronnie and Annette, you raised an amazing your lady. She was such an angel and will live on in my heart forever. Thank you for allowing me the opportunity to be her Coach. If I had one more day with Kayla I would tell her how much I love her and miss her. I would love to see her play basketball and watch her shoot 3s and say "I am on fire." I would want to give her a hug. She was such an affectionate person and she really had to work on me. Well, she broke me just as she did everyone who spent any time with her. I would try to make her laugh as much as possible because I miss that laugh so much. I would not let her leave again without telling her how much impact she had on my life while she was alive and how much her death has impacted me personally, professionally, and spiritually. K, if only we could have one more day.

Pondy (a name given to me by Kayla)
Coach Shelly Pond.

Letter from her nurse, Heather Haley

Dear Ronnie and Annette Watson, My name is Heather Haley. I am a nursing student at East Central University in Ada, Oklahoma. Me and my boyfriend were the second car to come upon your daughter's wreck. I am so sorry for your loss and I cannot imagine how broken your hearts are without her. I just wanted to write and let you know, that day changed my life forever.

The lady that arrived first and I knelt next your daughter and talked to her. I don't know if she could hear us, but I like to believe she could and that somehow we helped her feel calm and not alone. I have never felt so helpless in my life as I did that day waiting for the ambulance to arrive.

That night after this was over and I was home, I cried for all of you. For the boy who was driving, for you guys as her parents, for her friends. I, a total stranger, was with her at her most fragile moment. At that moment, you didn't what was going on. I heard that they got a hold of you later that night. Through this I realized how strong my passion for nursing really was. I want to help people and their families and treat them as if they were my own. I will never forget September 4, 2005 and I will never forget Kayla. I think of her often and pray for you every day.

God Bless you, Heather Haley

MEMORIES FROM FRIENDS

B est friends during her earthly years, these ladies shared their thoughts and memories of Kayla.

Alyssha Cox Walker:

She was the best friend anyone could ever ask for or have no matter how much time spent together. Even when she left for SWOSU, distance never mattered, nor did the amount of time that had passed since the last time we had seen each other. She still called me at least once a week to talk, whether it was just for two minutes to check up with each other or fill the other one in on something that was happening with ourselves or over an hour catching up in detail. It meant a lot to me at the time, but there aren't any words than can describe what it means to me, looking back on it, now. When I imagine her in my head, it's with that big, beautiful smile across her face. She was so easy to please, so content, so humble. Just driving the short distance to watch her play basketball in high school or college meant the world to her. As we all do, I adore her, love her and miss her so very much. I can't wait to have a copy of her story to read when I'm sad and I'm missing her.

Robin Dale:

I have so many memories of Kayla. I lay in bed some nights not being able to sleep because I'm thinking about how much I miss her and how great it would be to be able to talk to her again. I've always thought that after people die they get a better reputation than what they had when they were here. It's weird because we noticed how different she was. It didn't take losing her for her friends to notice. All the boys wanted to date her and all the girls wanted to be her friend. In fact, my high school boyfriend accidentally called me "Kayla" one time because he liked her. I should have been jealous but I knew what he saw in her. We all saw it. She carried God with her everywhere she went.

She was goofy and what a lot of people like to call "ornery." She put me up to things that only Kayla could have gotten me to do. I remember when she first talked to Sheena Smith at a basketball game. Sheena liked Matt Phillips and apparently didn't like Kayla for it. Of course, Kayla wasn't going to let someone "not like her." After she had played against her in basketball game she said, Come on rob, Let's go talk to Sheena." I had seen the daggers Sheena was throwing her from across the gym and wasn't exactly sure Kayla knew what she was getting herself into. I had never been in a fight before but I told her that I'd be backup because it looked like she was going to need it. Of course, Kayla had more strength in her one arm than I did in my whole entire body. We walked over and Kayla sat down next to Sheena and acted like she was her best friend. One of the first statements out of Kayla's mouth was "Man, I'm sweaty after that game. My armpits smell like biscuits." Matt likes you over me and you're talking about your armpits" It was all I could do to keep from laughing. The conversation ended with Kayla telling me she was going to get Sheena to go to church with her. You know how the story ended.

Sheena couldn't help but notice the same we all noticed. Kayla was always set apart from the rest of us because she was so good but somehow managed to make us feel like we were important.

Courtney Hill:

I met Kayla my freshman year of high school when she started school at Tushka. Even though we were officially meeting for the first time, I always knew the name Watson. They had a reputation for being amazing basketball players. Kayla was a remarkable basketball player but it did not define her. She carried a spirit with her that cannot be described. Before Kay came to Tushka, the popular thing to do was drink alcohol and smoke cigarettes, two things that Kayla never did. Seems so silly, but I remember thinking I wanted to be friends with those older girls who partied because they were the popular ones. That changed quickly after getting to know Kay. She completely changed the dynamics of the school. I would love to say that all the drinking and smoking stopped; it didn't. However, it wasn't the "thing" to do anymore. Kayla truly loved everyone and everyone loved her. She would not compromise in many areas of her life but she still was kind to those who did. Her idea of fun quickly became our idea of fun. I have never laughed as much as I did in the years I had with her. She could break the ice in any uncomfortable situation. She would make herself look like a fool if it meant making others laugh. Heck, she would get me to make a fool of myself too. I can't count the times she made me smell her underarms to see if they "smell like biscuits". She had a way about her that I have never seen in anyone else. Yes, she was an amazing basketball player. Yes, she was a diligent Christian. There was something else though. SHE was something else and I'll never stop missing her.

My friend, Marila writes

Kayla, It has almost been one year and I still can't completely grasp that fact that you are gone from this earth. I know where you are and that brings some comfort, because I know you are happy there. My cousin Stephanie passed away only 3 weeks before you and I'm sure she was waiting to welcome you into the gates of Heaven and only 6 months later I bet you both welcomed Monte's cousin Joe Wade into Heaven. They are both big cut ups so I know you will get along great. I miss you terribly. The source of the pain is not having you here, but my strength not only comes from Jesus but it also comes knowing you. In the time we spent together, you taught me determination and faith. That is now what I live by. I am determined to live a good life and work hard to succeed in it and I have the Faith that Jesus will never forsake me. Kayla thank you for AFFECTING my life. The moments we have shared will forever be cherished. I will carry these with me for the rest of my life. You are so amazing and I tell people about you often. I tell people about this fascinating girl who touched so many lives and who loved our Lord with all her heart. Kay I miss you so much but I'm just glad I was lucky enough to have God place YOU in my life. That's right God placed you in my life. He knew I needed you to teach me things that no one else could. You have shown me the way that I want to serve the Lord. I thank God for every second I had with you. I know someday we will be together again. I love you Kayla Beth!!! Love always, Marila

My little cousin, Kati Watson wrote this to me:

Kay,

This summer is almost over but for me it feels like it hasn't started yet. Every year we would all go to the lake and spend a little time together. This year without you it seems everyone was too busy. The lake is where you and I got closer and shared many laughs. Remember one year we were all at Lake Texoma playing volleyball and your dad was cutting up potatoes and my dad hit the ball way up in the air and it landed right in those potatoes? Everyone was just about on the ground laughing so hard . . . How about the time you brought out the T.V. so we could all watch a movie together? We watched "How to lose a guy in 10 days." Those were some good times . . . You always wanted to eat. But what Watson doesn't? Me, you, and Jen just about ate a whole chocolate cake by ourselves. Then we all had to put it in our teeth and take a picture. Oh, what about the time when me and you ran out of gas on your jet ski on the other side of the lake? People just drove by and waved at us. We swam and swam it seemed like forever, then this woman finally asked us if we needed help. You just kinda looked at me and smiled and was like, "Na, I think we'll swim the rest of the way." You didn't say that out loud. We laughed about till we got back to where we were camping . . . Then we would all camp at McGee. But this year it seemed like I was the only one that wanted to go. The last place you camped at McGee was the first spot on the left. I got there every time it was open. I camped out at the lake almost all summer long. But it just wasn't the same. A lot has happened this year at the lake but it doesn't compare with the times I shared with you there. You're on my mind every day, which you know you are. You are highly missed by me and many others. I love you so much. Thanks for hearing me when I really need it.

Love,
Kati

Jenny, the cousin who always made me laugh remembers:

Hey Kay I cannot even believe it has been 5 years. I remember like it was yesterday when we were at the lake and you woke me up saying let's go run. Or when we played volleyball and you kept saying service with a smile. Lol those were the days. I miss them so much. Remember when we were playing volleyball and Fudin hit the ball so high and it came down on the potatoes your mom was frying. We all bout peed our pants. I love telling Luke about those days. When Fudin made us run over the ducks when we were on the tube. Will never forget when you, Cass, Matt and I went running after Thanksgiving dinner and I got sick and had to ride the four wheeler home. Haha guess what? I'm still the same way. Harlee is almost 2 now and she is amazing. She is so hyper. Your neice is also amazing I love her to death. I think she looks just like your brother. Harlee thinks a lot about her. I wish you were here to see them and have one of your own too. Cassie's baby is getting so big. We are gonna have a little basketball team again. Maybe all three of the girls can go to the same school and become close friends. I can't wait to see Kayla. You are still a huge inspiration to a lot of people including me. I love you so much think about you every day. Jen

BIGFOOT EXPOSED

There had been some rumors of big foot sightings near our home. My dad and his brothers who had grown up on the creek banks were not buying it. They were discussing it when they suddenly came up with the idea to do their own big foot pictures that they would say came from game cameras placed in the area near recent sightings. They would not even tell their wives. It was to be top secret mission and pictures would go to the local newspaper only. So, Dad and Matt got a bear hide from the taxidermy shop and went behind the house to snap a couple of pictures that would soon capture the media nationwide. Dad developed the pictures and dropped them by his brother's store and tells the clerk that the pictures are not to leave the store, but to be given only to his brother. The brother in question wishes to remain anonymous so for the purpose of this story the brother will be referred to by the pseudonym, Toad. Toad was to give the pictures to the *Atoka County Times*. However, the clerk allowed someone to take a picture of the photos using a camera on a cell phone and the rest is history.

Within hours, the photos were on the internet and the media was hounding. Toad had initially agreed to be the "media spokesman," but, again, he had only planned to deal with local media only. When Channel 12, Channel 10, Daily Oklahoman and CNN started calling, Toad turned his phone off, changed the code to his gate and told my dad, "I'm out, don't you give my number to anyone." Then, Searcingforbigfoot.com hunters came. They allegedly found some fruit and a lean-to that big foot had discarded, but before big foot could be apprehended there was another sighting near Paris, TX, and the search crew left to chase him. Dad found it amazing that fruit could be found during the bad drought we had that summer. They had no idea how serious people take big foot sightings. It put Caney on the map I guess.

FROM THE "FAM"

My dad's brother, Keith "Pig" Watson wrote this poem to me. He could be a little gruff and considered an outlaw maybe, but I loved him just the same. No matter where I saw him I always had a hug for him. One day he was at my dad's shop and I went out and gave him a bible. He wrote me this poem and it was so touching. You would just have to know him to really appreciate how special this poem really was.

God needed an angel on earth August 16, 1984
To spread His word and lead souls through heaven's door,
God's angel was Kayla, true heart and loving face,
Kayla went to work for God at a rapid pace,
With Kayla's true heart, loving face and sweet smile
She touched many lives in just a little while.
Kayla liked the challenge and competition in every way,
But God's word she never did stray.
September 4, 2005 God called His angel home through heaven's door
With Kayla's true heart reaching out there will be many more,
Though God's angel was only with us a short while,
Kayla was waiting for her loved ones in Heaven
With true heart, loving face and sweet smile

My mom asked my dad and my brothers to write me a letter for this book.

This is the letter from Dad:

Kayla,

If you were here I would drink any concoction you could mix up. I would give you all my change and you wouldn't even have to look for where it was hid. In fact, I would give all my worldly possessions just to have you back for one day. I would let you burn me out in the car while your vent was off. I would buy you every copy of "Hope Floats" and watch it endlessly with you. I would cook you pancakes again. You always loved me to cook pancakes after your ball games. I wouldn't wake you up on days that you didn't have practice. I would let you aggravate me to death and would laugh along with you. Remember, when you and Mom thought it was so funny to take that short cut from Ada. It was pouring down rain and we nearly ran out of gas because you guys kept saying you knew the short cut and you had us in the middle of nowhere in the country in the middle of the night. You two wouldn't stop laughing while I am saying, "Oh, it's going to be really funny when we are lost and out of gas." That would just make you roar more. Then, Mom would say "oh, I know where we are. Turn here," which would be another dead end. I guess we drove over an hour lost in that storm before I finally figured out how to get back to Ada and go the long way home. Kayla, if you were here I would definitely want to take the long way home. No shortcuts. I would enjoy every moment. It seems like I was so busy working when you were here. I didn't get to be with you as much as I wanted. I regret that. Mom says that was why I want to have Kayden here all the time, so I don't miss a thing. I sure miss you and am looking forward to the day when we meet again and won't have to worry about saying goodbye.

A letter from my little brother, Matt:

Sis,

One of my first memories of you is of you going to school and I would cry to go with you. I even got on the bus once when Mom wasn't looking. When I started in kindergarten, I remember you walking me to my classroom before you went to your class. I remember us building tree houses, swimming, and of course playing basketball. Remember the little foam goal that we would hang on the door inside and we would play all the time. Dad would swear we were going to tear the house down. He finally poured us a court outside and this would be a place of many intense battles. I remember you changing schools and going to Stringtown and I would stay behind at Caney. Then Mom said it was too hard to have us at two different schools and you talked me into going to Stringtown. After we moved there I loved it. Then, you decide to move to Tushka. I wanted to stay at Stringtown, but if that wasn't an option I would go back to Caney. I went to Caney for one day. The next day I found out that for you to be eligible to play ball I had to go with you to Tushka. I really hated changing schools again and especially starting a new school, but I did it for you. I think I got a new four wheeler out of the deal too. I ended up going to three different schools that week. I am pretty sure that I set some kind of sixth grade record because in one week I had played on three different basketball teams. Luke Howard teased Mom that I carried three suits in my bag and would change at halftime. I eventually felt at home at Tushka and was happy there.

The funniest memory I have of you was when we would play this game we made up we called cheek pinchers and we would grab each other's mouth and see who could stretch the farthest and stand the pain the longest. I could never beat you at this.

When the call came about the accident, it just didn't seem real. I couldn't believe it. It started to sink in when we saw you at the hospital. Then for some reason, I drove my own vehicle to family night. Afterwards, I remember coming home and sitting in my truck and just crying so hard as the reality that you were gone began to sink in.

At the service I remember Emily singing the "Running" song you liked and Matt Phillips' eulogy. Mom and Dad had asked me before the service did we want to receive the line of mourners or did I think we should exit before afraid that it would be too exhausting. I made the decision that we should greet the people. It was exhausting but still nice to be able to share with all the people that loved you. I couldn't believe how many people were there. Our friends from Stringtown were there. Preston, Orlando and CJ came and talked to me and that meant a lot to me. I think you would really have liked the service but it was sad, and depressing to me to say goodbye to my big sister.

I don't talk about the wreck much. I think it was your time and that it was in God's hands. I remember you wanting me to fix the seat belts in Chance's pickup so that you could sleep during the ride home. We talk about our memories of you. Every day I think of you.

How my life has changed since you been gone? I think that I have been able to move forward. I married Monise and we have two little girls. We named our first one after you, Kayden Elizabeth. She is three now and has your big brown eyes. We also have Kambreigh Mae who is 8 months old. I think you would be a great aunt. I wish that you were here so that we could have kids that could grow up together. I miss not getting to share that with you.

What I would do if I could spend one more day with you? Of course, I would beat you in a game of 21 first. Since, I last saw you I have grown about five inches. You don't have a height advantage anymore. Plus, I have gained about 50 pounds. I work out all the time and eat healthy like you used to do. After I beat you in basketball, we would go run. You loved to run and so do I. Remember the time we ran to midway church, six miles away. If you were here we could enter a marathon. That would be fun. I would want you to meet my family and my kids. Then we would just spend time doing whatever you wanted to do just as long as we were together, but first I would beat you in basketball, lol.

The thing I regret most about our life together was that I wish I had seen you more after you left for college. I should have spent more time with you. I remember once just a few months before the accident that Mom let me miss school to go and see you at college. It was a long weekend so I got to stay a few days there. We played volleyball, basketball and Nintendo. You took me everywhere and we had the best time together. You introduced me to all your friends. I wish that I had taken the time to do that more. You loved having me there. You would always ask Mom, "Do you think he will come back?" You were the best big sister.

I think losing you has made me a stronger person. It was so hard to get past it at first, but I finally learned how to deal with it. I had already lost my best friend, Jimmy Braziell, both of my grandpas and then you. After losing all these loved ones, it has somewhat hardened my heart, but out of all of these, yours is the worst. I sure miss you a lot and sometimes when I run I just break down and cry. I try my best to keep it hid from everyone because I hate for Mom and Dad or even Monise to see me cry. It just makes *me feel weak. I am really looking forward to the day when I get to see you again. It was going to be such a happy day. I love ya!*

From James

I miss you sis. Mom asked me to write a letter to you for the book and all I can think of is how much I miss you. I have no bad memories of you. From the first time I met you at the adoption party you were nice to me. After I was adopted, you had already gone to college. I wish that I had gotten adopted earlier and could have grown up with you like Matt did. I remember that you were always happy to call me your brother and didn't care that I was black. I also remember that you never left the house even if you were going on a date that you didn't ask me to go along. Most of the time, I didn't but you always made me feel welcome. That is just how sweet you were to me. I was so happy to be your brother. I remember the day you left and I hugged you goodbye. I hugged you so hard and begged you to stay. You said you had to leave. There was something special about the hug though. It is like we knew but we didn't know that we were saying goodbye for awhile.

I wish you could have been here to watch us win state twice and to see me play in college. I think you would have been my biggest fan. I know that I love you and wear your number to honor you.

Do you have any idea how hard it is to grow up in a family that had you and Matt before me? I could never fill your shoes and I am not sure I even tried. But, somehow we made it work and I am really happy to have a wonderful family.

I am going to graduate college this year. Can you believe that? I know you would be happy about that. I am trying to make my family proud sis and someday I promise I will see you in heaven. Your baby brother, James

Mom's closing remarks:

King Solomon wrote in Ecclesiastes that "people cannot see the whole scope of God's work from beginning to end" and I would agree. We live our lives in forward motion, but only understand when we look back. Then we can see how the threads contribute to the weaving of very large and beautiful tapestry. We see things and think of them in isolation. When we consider the entire sequence of events it becomes miraculous. We look back at what were difficult times in Kayla's life such as having no friends and changing schools. At the time we didn't understand, but in looking back it was God's plan because she had more people to reach and lives to influence. Each part of her life is now woven into a beautiful tapestry. A wonderfully designed quilt made by God.

Kayla's heroes were the young people including, Cassie Bernall and Rachel Scott who lived out their faith and offered their lives for their faith in the Columbine shooting. She loved how their stories were reaching others and strengthen faith in others after their sudden, tragic deaths. Although Kayla would not be considered a martyr like them she was a hero of faith. She never compromised. She carried God and His mission with her all her life. I want to live like that. I want to give it all I have got. I know that it was never proper to speak evil of the dead and sometimes people become saints after their death as we tend to remember the good and overlook the bad. That was not the case with Kayla. She always had such a kind heart. I always told her she was too good for this world. What I loved most about her was her pure heart and how committed she was to God. I loved the maturity and responsibility she always showed. I loved how compassionate and caring she was to others especially to the elderly and poor. I loved how she always made me feel loved and wanted. I will always be humbled and honored that she called me "Mom."

Here are some notes from my (Kayla) personal bible studies and journals that I left behind:

> He's not keeping a record of your mistakes or the time you blew.
> His blood will take care of those things, your mistakes. All he sees is you.
> His love and desire for you aren't based on what you do for him but on who He was.
> He must become greater, I must become less.
> Enjoying God that was what Christianity was all about.
> Written on the cover of my last journal: The Lord will fulfill his purpose for me.

I was reading "The Purpose Driven Life" again and made these notes:

> Day 1. *It all starts with God. It's not about you. The purpose of your life was far greater than your own personal fulfillment, your peace of mind or even your happiness. You were born by His purpose and for his purpose.*
>
> *You didn't create yourself so there's no way you can tell yourself what you were created for. Focusing on ourselves will never reveal life's purposes.*
>
> 1. *You discover our identity and purpose through a relationship with Jesus Christ.*
>   *God was thinking of you long before you ever thought about him. You may choose your career, spouse, your hobbies, and many parts of your life, but you don't get to choose your purpose.*

2. *God was thinking of you long before you ever thought about him. You may choose your career, spouse, your hobbies and many parts of your life, but you don't get to choose your purpose.*

   The purpose of your life fits into a much larger, cosmic purpose that God has designed for eternity. Colossians 1:16

Day 2. *You are not an Accident. It was not fate, nor chance, nor luck, nor coincidence that you are breathing at this very moment. The Lord will fulfill his purpose for me! Psalms 138:8*

My obituary contained these words that came from the last page of the journal I made for Mom.

A few words from Kayla

The happiest of people don't necessarily have the best of everything; they just make the most of all that comes their way. We should all imitate these people who have learned to live with what life has allotted them. By deciding to be content with whatever comes along, one will learn to look for good in every situation.

I trust that God orders my steps so I depend on Him to work out His plan. If you aren't moving forward with God then you are drifting backward. You are as close to God as you want to be. Take it one day at a time.

If my life were to end today, I would have to say that I have had a blessed life. I have grown in every difficult situation and all the things have worked out for the best in my life.

Love,
Kayla

A FEW WORDS FROM HEAVEN

Dear family and friends,

I am home. I am where I belong. I want to let you know a few things about my life now. First of all, at my accident, my soul peeled itself away from my body. I felt released. I felt no pain as my spirit left before my body before it absorbed any pain. There was absolutely no fear at the time of my death. There was grace for dying just as there was grace for everything. I felt nothing but overwhelming peace and comfort. If you are a Christian, when you die you are immediately in the presence of Christ where there was fullness of joy (Psalms 16:11)

The poem, *"The Ship" (Edwards)* describes my arrival to heaven.

The Ship

I am standing upon the seashore and see a nearby ship spread her white sails to the morning breeze and start for the blue ocean.

She was an object of beauty and strength. I watch until at length she was only a speck of white cloud just where the sea and sky meet and mingle. Then someone at my side exclaims, "She's gone!"

Gone where? Gone from my sight, that was all. She was just as large in hull and mast and spar as she was when she departed and just as able to bear her load of living freight to the place of her destination. Her diminished size was in me, not in her.

And just at the moment when someone cries, "she's gone, there are other eyes watching for her arrival, and other voices that take up the glad shout, "there she comes."

And that was dying

-Author unknown.

Hebrews 12:1 says "therefore, since we are surrounded by so great a cloud of witnesses." This welcoming committee was wildly cheering for me as I approached the finish line. I saw my papa Jack, my papa Harley, Paula Huffman with Abbie Delay, my cousin, Larry Rose, Sean Hall and so many more applauding passionately for me and running to embrace me.

My arrival caused such celebration. I felt nothing but love and joy as we danced, hugged and greeted each other. Nothing compares to when I met My FATHER who said "well done, my good and faithful servant. You have not labored in vain." (Matthew 25:21)

I loved my life on earth but heaven so much richer in color and intense beauty. Our vocabulary was just not rich enough to describe the experience in a way that was understandable to the human mind. Jesus called it paradise and it truly was. It was the Garden of Eden restored. All of heaven was celebrating my arrival. I was drinking in the beauty and rejoicing with my family and friends. The bible described heaven like this:

Revelation 21:4 *He will wipe away every tear from their eyes, and death shall be no more, neither shall there be mourning, nor crying, nor pain anymore, for the former things have passed away."*

What I can tell you about heaven is that there is no suffering here. There is no cancer, there are no hungry children, there are no orphans, and there are no lonely or hurting people. There are no more goodbyes. There are no battles against satanic forces here. God makes everything new here. The wound in my momma's heart will finally be completely healed.

> **Revelation 22:1-5** *Then the angel showed me the river of the water of life, bright as crystal, flowing from the throne of God and of the Lamb through the middle of the street of the city; also, on either side of the river, the tree of life with its twelve kinds of fruit, yielding its fruit each month. The leaves of the tree were for the healing of the nations. No longer will there be anything accursed, but the throne of God and of the Lamb will be in it, and his servants will worship him. They will see his face, and his name will be on their foreheads. And night will be no more. They will need no light of lamp or sun, for the Lord God will be their light, and they will reign forever and ever.*

Yes, there really are streets of gold, huge mansions built just for us and the river of life is here. It is just like it was in the Garden of Eden. The tree of life is here too. Meaning we will never die. We will spend all eternity in this wonderful place. It is such a beautiful place. There is nothing but clear, sunny days. I haven't seen a tear. We are having a great time. Wish you were here. I hope you join me here. I am saving a special place just for you. The only way you get to come is if you know Christ as your savior.

God says in order to go to Heaven, you must be born again. In John 3:7, Jesus said to Nicodemus, "Ye must be born again." In the Bible, God gives us the plan of how to be born again which means to be saved. His plan is simple!

First, you must realize you are a sinner. "For all have sinned, and come short of the glory of God." (Romans 3:23)

Because you are a sinner, you are condemned to death. "For the wages [payment] of sin is death" (Romans 6:23). This includes eternal separation from God in Hell. "It was appointed unto men once to die, but after this the judgment" (Hebrews 9:27). But God loved you so much He gave His only begotten Son, Jesus, to bear your sin and die in your place."

"God commendeth His love toward us, in that, while we were yet sinners, Christ died for us" (Romans 5:8).

In Acts 16:30-31, the Philippian jailer asked Paul and Silas: ". . . 'Sirs, what must I do to be saved?' And they said, 'Believe on the Lord Jesus Christ, and thou shalt be saved . . .'"

Then, simply believe on Him as the one who bore your sin, died in your place, was buried, and whom God resurrected. His resurrection powerfully assures that the believer can claim everlasting life when Jesus was received as Savior.

"For whosoever shall call upon the name of the Lord shall be saved." (Romans 10:13).

If you haven't made that decision before please do it now. Right now, wherever you are, repenting, lift your heart to God in prayer.

Just pray: "Oh God, I know I am a sinner. I believe Jesus was my substitute when He died on the Cross. I believe His shed blood, death, burial, and resurrection were for me. I now receive Him as my Savior. I thank You for the forgiveness of my sins, the gift of salvation and everlasting life, because of Your merciful grace. Amen."

God's power will save you, keep you saved, and enable you to live a victorious Christian life. After you are saved, there are some things you should practice daily for spiritual growth:

Pray—you talk with God.
Read your Bible—God talks to you.
Witness—share your faith with others

Find a good bible believing church that will help you grow and teach you things about our Father.

I am so happy that you made that decision. I will be praying for you and cheering you on as you complete your journey. Remember, the only way you lose was to quit. So, if you stumble and fall, get back up. Never quit. Trust me; you don't want to miss out on this. I miss you.

Love Kayla

BIBLIOGRAPHY

The Ache We Hold Inside. TCF Cincinnati Chapter Newsletter: Feb. 1993. Web. <http://www.oocities.org/tcfalbuquerque/writings.htm>

Edwards, Gene. *Dear Lillian.* Auburn: Seedsowers, 1991. Print.

Holy Bible: New International Version. Grand Rapids, MI: Zondervan, 2011. Print.

Lewis, Clive Staples. *A Grief Observed.* San Francisco: HarperOne, 2001. Print.

ABOUT THE AUTHOR

A NNETTE WATSON grew up in Caney, Oklahoma and married Ronnie Watson in 1983. They made a wonderful life for themselves in the country, in southeast Oklahoma, where they raised four beautiful children, two by birth, Kayla and Matt (25) and two by adoption, James (21) and Charisma (9). Annette also has a wonderful stepdaughter, Kary Watson Johnson of Dallas, TX. Annette spent fifteen years working for the Oklahoma Department of Human Services (DHS) in the Child Protection Division, and has recently become a Licensed Professional Counselor (LPC). Her dedication to children's welfare, whether her own or someone else's, is a recognizable and tremendous effort.

Life was wonderful until tragedy struck, when a car accident instantly took the life of her beloved daughter, Kayla, in 2004. Kayla was 21 at the time, and on her way back to college at SWOSU in Weatherford, OK, where she played basketball. Through Annette's heartfelt words, you will experience Kayla's life and legacy of faith as well as learning how God's grace helped their family survive the unimaginable pain of having a child "Go Home Early."

CPSIA information can be obtained at www.ICGtesting.com
Printed in the USA
LVOW052334010513

331856LV00001B/3/P